DEATH
BY
LIVING

DEATH BY LIVING

N. D. WILSON

THOMAS NELSON
Since 1798

NASHVILLE   DALLAS   MEXICO CITY   RIO DE JANEIRO

Published in Nashville, Tennessee, by Thomas Nelson. Thomas Nelson is a registered trademark of Thomas Nelson, Inc.

Author is represented by the literary agency of Aaron Rench, Leaptide Literary Group.

Thomas Nelson, Inc., titles may be purchased in bulk for educational, business, fund-raising, or sales promotional use. For information, please e-mail SpecialMarkets@ThomasNelson.com.

Scripture quotations marked ESV are from THE ENGLISH STANDARD VERSION. © 2001 by Crossway Bibles, a division of Good News Publishers.

Scripture quotations marked KJV are from the King James Version.

ISBN 978-0-7852-3837-9 (IE)

Library of Congress Data Available Upon Request

ISBN 978-0-8499-2009-7

Printed in the United States of America

13 14 15 16 17 18 RRD 6 5 4 3 2 1

For my Lovely,

in her eyes, the sun is always on the water.

Contents

CONTENTS

Introduction: Hello Again

Background

Way back yonder, in 2008, I wrote my first book-length chunk of nonfiction. It was a whirly-gig called *Notes from the Tilt-a-Whirl*, and it was my best effort to paint a way of seeing, of peering behind the curtains of creation, a way of listening and laughing and loving the craziness of the reality in which we all live. It was an outworking of years of reading and wrangling, of classroom scuffles and pub chats, a pent-up accumulation that came out like a raucous philosophy of religion course married to a nice, wholesome happy hour (with two-dollar drafts). That book was my manifesto of faith.

This is a spoken world—from galaxies to inchworms, from seraphs to electrons to meter maids, every last thing was and is shaped *ex nihilo*. It—and we—all exist as beats and rhythms and rhymes in the cosmic and constant word art of the Creator God. To fully embrace and attempt to apply such a vision is . . . dizzying. In *Notes*, I did my best. But there is more to be said. More angles to capture. More spinning to be spun.

Title

Rewind. In 2005, years before *Notes*, I wrote a short essay entitled "Death by Living." I have actually been writing for this book since that moment, some of which I used elsewhere, some of which I have heavily updated and reused here, some of which I have simply chucked. Because this book is thematically shaped around phases of life and time, I also really enjoyed dipping into some of my older writing and getting a glimpse of my young expressions of ideas that were (at the time) new discoveries for me. I had forgotten how raw I was (and somehow found less insight in my younger self than I *most definitely* remember having). Regardless, that original, very short "Death by Living" essay was a seed in my life, and the title became a slogan for Team Wilson (my wife and me) as we poured the sloppy concrete foundation of our young family and began encountering the real business of life.

A midnight flu of heroic proportions sweeps through

the house after a generous dinner of saucy meatball subs. We shake kids' sheets out off the front porch, grimacing and mouth-breathing all the while. (I actually tossed one crib sheet into the bushes and simply walked away.) My wife looks at me and laughs out the line, even through a gag.

"Death by living."

Rugged childbirth. Smile. Death by living. Back surgery. Hydrocodone withdrawals. A last-minute and completely farcical road trip from London to Rome with nine young cousins in a van. Death by living. Being robbed in Rome upon arrival. Death by living. Scars, wrinkles, bruises, weariness, grief and joy and exhaustion; we've come by it all honestly—by being alive.

Notes from the Tilt-a-Whirl focuses on a way of seeing. With this book, the focus is on a way of living, a way of receiving life. There are, of course, many ways in which these two things are deeply entangled and impossible to separate, so don't bother trying. It's a matter of emphasis. I am a man attempting to paint another picture of the same wonderful world, but I have turned my easel around. I've taken my best shot at the sunrise. Now for the sunset.

Here, in this painting, in these (hopefully) creative meditations, you will see the same sky and the same sun, the same story of struggle, of fall and grace, of descent and ascent, of death and resurrection. The same God. The same gifts. If He's not tired of it, why should I be? If His brush is still in His hand, if His words still roll, what can I do but stick my tongue out the corner of my mouth and diligently (but pitifully) rip Him off? What can I do but meditate on His meditations?

Shape, Tone, & Gratitude

Lastly, *Notes* was built around seasonal spinning. This book hangs on a creature's narrative motion through time (past, present, and future) and is (slightly) more linear. But not Euclid linear, not pencil-tucked-up-against-a-ruler linear. This book is linear like my novels are linear, like a river (with rapids and falls and rocks and eddies and chutes) is linear, the linear of a long, sea-heaving wave rolling its thundering shore-pound up the coast.

Grab a rented raft, hop in the rinkiest-dinkiest sea kayak you can find. Pull on a puffy orange life vest and buckle it (rather awkwardly) between your legs. Brandish your paddle. Ignore all sunscreen. By the time we're done, you'll be chafed in such new and innovative ways that the familiarity of a sunburn just might be a comfort, a little tingling reassurance that you are still you.

Lastly-lastly, I need to thank my father and my mother for their way of life. They handed me Chesterton and read me Lewis. They've never flinched at the cost of truly living, of being mortal. This year, my mother lost her father. Last year, my father lost his mother. I groped for words beside two deep holes awaiting two broken bodies—two vessels of flesh and life and story that had been used up and cast off in the way they were intended to be.

Inspiration

There are authors and thinkers I could rattle off in the background of this book, like a waiter describing today's special. I could throw out a pile of nice thinky literary names (arugula, saffron, duck fat), and they would all be genuine influences on everything I say and how I say it. But the truth is this: the need that I have to write this book, the deep itch that must be scratched comes from having said a young man's good-byes to my own flesh and blood, from having planted two more stones in the Easter garden.

Elizabeth Catherine Dodds Wilson. Lawrence Aubry Greensides.

They rest in peace. I spring from their roots.

Meditation

That's what I'll be doing—meditating. Pull up a yoga mat (beside me on the beach). Those of you capable of crossing your legs, feel free. I'll bonfire the incense—a little blend I call hunk of wet cedar, sand grass, old s'more, lighter fluid, and lost shoe. Oh, and for me, meditation is a noisy, noisy business. There's a chance of hard cider, and a likelihood of shouting.

Places, Every*%&&##body

YOO-HOO.

Psst, hey.

Guy in the tapered corduroys with the flapjack butt, catechumen of cool, keeper of your generation's two and a half original thoughts—I'd like to speak with you.

And you, all-natural gluten-less girl, lover of things shade grown, shedder of tears for unseen chickens, lesser priestess of the Cruelty-Free, defender of the helpless (excluding womb-dwellers).

And you, guy in the belted khakis, young republican't, worshipper of the imaginary (secular but holy) American Financial Fertility Goddess.

And you, mother of seven, snarling at the back rows in your extendo-van.

And you, masturbatory middle-aged gym poser, leering past your own veiny reflection at the girl on the rowing machine.

And you, Christian youth, straddler of two stools, devotee of an unambitious god who wants only to serve as the figurehead of your personal aorta (graciously leaving the rest to your peers).

Athletes and worship leaders and cheaters, fathers and sons and mothers and daughters.

You.

Abused or abuser. Lost or repentant, wandering or rooted, germ cultures of pride or of self-loathing.

Ahoy, the numb and the debauched (or both).

You.

The faithful.

You.

The faithless.

Pause.

Shut your eyes. Inhale slowly. Now hold that breath while your eyes open. Assess your position before you exhale, between your last breath and the next. Start simply. Where are you?

On a park bench? A bus seat? The john? In a secondhand archaic armchair alone in a seventeenth-hand apartment? Where are you exactly on this planet? How many feet above sea level and how many feet below and above the nearest stars? Where are you in time, in history, in the beyond-all-human-comprehension parade of handcrafted matter marching in noise and glory through this thing we call the present moment?

Please provide me with your physical, temporal, genealogical, historical, narratival, and spiritual coordinates, because I want to know you (not personally, just as a viewer, thanks). I'm coming to your story at least halfway through the show, and I missed seasons one through seventy-four. I'm flipping through a novel thicker than the General Sherman (on onion skin paper too), and I can't find you or your dadgum moment.

How far are you from your birth? No, let me try flipping backward from the end. How close are you to your death? Help me find your narrative.

"Story, story, my life is a story," says the hipster to his Twitter feed.

Right. Narrative. Story. Boy, it sounds nice and groovy, but it's coming from someone who barely has enough of an attention span to get through a Web clip of over four minutes, and may the postmodern gods show their mercy if the atmospheric WiFi wanes or his little browser starts buffering.

No matter how trendy it might be when some people say it, life *is* a story. All of history is a story. Every particle has its own story trailing backward until it reaches the first Word of the One and Three, and all of those trailing threads— those many—are woven into the one great ever-growing divinely spoken narrative.

In other words, no matter how trite we might be, no matter how much we might use the idea to inflate our own perception of our own personal autonomous self-worth, no matter how much we might swank about in trend-appropriate glasses and trend-appropriate jeans, flexing *Story* like that one word and the thoughtfulness it implies is all the mojo we could ever need. We are, in fact, on to something. Each of us is in the middle of a story.

But for some reason, we don't show the slightest desire to read it, let alone live it with any kind of humble self-awareness.

Some people see the huge swirl of history—the impossibly numerous narrative threads always rolling toward the beach in one incomprehensibly massive wave, and they make one large theological assumption posing as a conclusion (it's all just too much, even for the God speaking it all), and then they climb up into the pulpit to issue an utterance for those among us who might be too simple or naïve to have noticed the bigness of reality.

"How dare you thank God after you win a football game. Do you really think He cares?"

"How dare you pray before your event at the Olympics and get all pious after victory. Do you think God doesn't like the other girls?"

Some people see only the swirl of their immediate surroundings, and then only in a radius of inches. Life is a story. I'm a superstar. Get out of my way, I'm busy starring in this little thing I like to call Me. Which, Mom, you clearly don't understand. Headphones firmly on . . .

On the one hand, people assume that God is diffident and distant, with all the personality of the Great Gray Yawn in the Sky. On the other, people act like God is their personal gnome of narrative manipulation.

Ready, set, chop the baby.

The world is big, yes. But God is bigger. Yes, your life is a story, but you are carpet-dwelling, dust-mite teensy on the scale of this stage, and number only one in the multitude of His cast.

Your world is tiny, yes. But God gets tinier. Not one dust mite falls through the carpet fibers and into the pad apart from your Father. He's big enough that *small* doesn't matter. Dust-mite drama doesn't use up His attention, taking it away from something deemed by mentally incontinent college professors to be more worthy of His attention. When one is infinite, one can enjoy two black holes arm-wrestling over a galactic snack, and an uncoordinated junior high quarterback struggling to escape an overweight junior high defensive end. Infinite goes all the way up and all the way down; and at every level, with equal attention, He creates with the full dose of His personality.

Job of Uz: Why?

The Whirlwind: Did you clothe the hipster and give him his coffee and inverted brand fascination?

A drought in the Midwest and a hawk chasing a crow

are both scenes that hold His attention. They are not things that happen which He then may or may not notice . . . He speaks and crafts every piece of matter woven into those scenes, and that is why they happen. His speaking is their happening.

Understand this: we are both tiny and massive. We are nothing more than molded clay given breath, but we are nothing less than divine self-portraits, huffing and puffing along mountain ranges of epic narrative arcs prepared for us by the Infinite Word Himself. Swell with pride and gratitude, for you are tiny and given much. You are as spoken by God as the stars. You stand in history with stories stretching out both behind and before. We should want to live our chapters well, but doing so requires that we know the chapters that led up to us in our time and our moment; it requires that we open our eyes and consciously begin to shape those chapters that are coming after.

Those who love to talk about *Story* rarely attempt to read much past their own immediate moment, and that not well. But it's hard to blame them. Try it. You have already held your breath and looked around yourself. Wherever you are, it is a scene, a location, a setting. How did you get there? Why are you there? What are you supposed to be doing? If you were imaginary, and you could read your scene in a book, you would have an easier time answering. Get outside your own head and your own little decisions and read the story. How did you get here? You can't really know where you should be going next, until you've taken a look at the road behind you.

Unhinge your jaw; struggle to read and learn and speak God's story of yourself after Him, that story in which you live. Know that you have a better chance of spewing out the Snake River than of telling your full story well. But not trying is the shortest route to character failure.

Clear your throat and open your eyes. You are on stage. The lights are on. It's only natural if you're sweating, because this isn't make-believe. This is theater for keeps. Yes, it is a massive stage, and there are millions of others on stage with you. Yes, you can try to shake the fright by blending in. But it won't work. You have the Creator God's full attention, as much attention as He ever gave Napoleon. Or Churchill. Or even Moses. Or billions of others who lived and died unknown. Or a grain of sand. Or one spike on one snowflake. You are spoken. You are seen. It is your turn to participate in creation. Like a kindergartener shoved out from behind the curtain during his first play, you might not know which scene you are in or what comes next, but God is far less patronizing than we are. You are His art, and He has no trouble stooping.

You can even ask Him for your lines.

—— T W O ——

Soul Food, Paper Boats, and the Pitcher: Stories Told

I AM ALONE IN MY BED, STUDYING THE LEGO WAR THAT I have left frozen on the floor, listening to the washing machine rumble on the other side of my bedroom/laundry room, waiting for my mother. A homemade stick-horse is watching me from the corner (a large brown velveteen head was mom-sewn over a hockey stick). A mom-sewn hot-air balloon is hanging from my low lean-to ceiling (despite the fact that the balloon occasionally and nightmarishly becomes a giant's head looming above me). I am accompanied in my bed by a stubby rhino (that will eventually inspire a creature in my 100 Cupboards trilogy), a lopsided killer whale packed with incredibly dense stuffing (deadly

9

in pillow fights and eventually banned), and Billy, a soft bear with odd ears and a speckled gray sweat suit sewn for him by my mother.

Tonight, as I look back from some two and a half decades later, that killer whale is in my basement, the rhino is in the attic with four sleepers, and Billy is sleeping beside my two-year-old daughter. He's still wearing that sweat suit.

On that long-ago night (and on many others like it), those animals and I were waiting for a story.

It was a small house, but my sisters' bedroom was on the far side of it. I could hear muffled voices and laughs that would eventually lead to footsteps that would eventually lead to me. My father sang and prayed over all of us and read us our first Lewis and Tolkien at the dinner table, but at bedtime, my mother was the storyteller. When she stepped (one step) down into my room and sat on my bed, there were two things that I would immediately request—a back rub and a story about Tiny Tim.

I don't remember any of the stories. My mother is relieved that I don't, sure that they would be embarrassing now (they wouldn't be). But I do remember the hum of the washing machine, the rattle of the dryer, and the deep thrill of getting what I wanted—of setting off on a trek with my friend Tim, who was no taller than my finger.

Stories are soul food. I fed on those stories, sending my imagination wandering as sleep took me, just as much as I fed on the classics of fantasy and adventure that my father read to us at the dinner table. As much as the stories of war and farms and trains that I heard from my grandfathers. As much as I fed on a short book my father wrote for me (and starring me), in which I accidentally killed a goblin king with my baseball bat while walking home from a game and got myself sucked into an underworld.

Growth requires food. Multiple times every day, throughout my entire childhood, I was fed. How many specific meals do I remember? How many peanut butter and jelly sandwiches do I remember uniquely as distinct from all the others? I remember meals in the same way that I remember story times. The atmosphere and aura of feeding—goblets and goblins, milk and villains, ice cream and orcs. I was fed. I grew. Inside and out. We are narrative creatures, and we need narrative nourishment—narrative catechisms.

Tiny Tim and I did some great things together. (Ask Billy; he remembers.)

For years, all we do is feed. We don't control what our parents feed us for dinner, we don't control what they read to us (or don't read to us) or what they let us watch. We are like jars of wet clay, and we are loaded full with every kind of tale—films; books; TV shows; stories from friends, parents, grandparents. And as we dry, we take the shape of what has been dumped inside of us. When we begin to make our own choices, when we become an active character in our own narratives, all of that soul food is behind us. We might not even remember the stories, but they groomed and molded us while we were still unfired clay.

Even in adults, stories groom instincts, and instincts control loyalties, and loyalties shape choices. But growth is harder for adults.

And then we move beyond just making our own choices. We begin deciding what narratives we will pour (or allow to be poured) into our own small people. We will feed them. Or, far more frequently, others will do it for us.

Souls will be fed and shaped from the inside out. That much is inescapable.

My children haven't heard a thing about Tiny Tim. But they do know Tiny Sinbad. He's the one who collects their lost teeth (leaving money and a tiny grateful note explaining what he plans on carving with the human ivory). And when they were still too young to be reading books on their own and (mostly) too squirrelly to sit still while I read to them, we started a tradition. Almost.

Bedtime. As a character in her own story, my mother taught me how rich that twilight of wakefulness could be. At night, I had four pairs of young eyes and four eagerly bouncing young souls waiting for me in three beds and one crib. (And Billy.)

I had to try. What kind of hypocrite would I be otherwise? Stories are my job. And surely my own children deserved my best stuff? Well, too bad. Because stories are hard.

These days, three can read and the fourth is well underway. Only little number five begs for stories in the way they all used to. Three devour novels in their beds, the fourth devours my old *Calvin and Hobbes*, and the fifth is entirely dependent on others for her narrative grub. But it isn't hard to remember when there were just four, and they were all baby birds, squalling for a story.

Slide time back into an older present. I walk upstairs to the room that holds four beds that hold four children. They never think they're tired, these four. Their eyes are bright and their young minds crackle with surprising thoughts on the day, the future, the nature of the universe. I am here to bid them farewell, to break little bottles of champagne on little bows, to let go of four imaginations and send them floating alone through the darkness, unchaperoned, unguided, shaping visions for themselves, resting in warmth or wandering into terror.

Every night, I feel like I'm launching paper boats into an ocean. I point these children as best I can. I flavor their minds with subjects and characters and songs and dances and blessings. And when they are warm and spilling over with joy, I let go, and I wait for the morning to hear of their adventures.

This is why we sing about drunken sailors and what to do with them, about how some folks say a man is made out of mud, about lost Scottish love and the walls of Jerusalem. This is why I must tell them stories.

In those early days, when story nights came, I would gather them around the youngest brother (still in crib captivity), and I would tell them some fatherly version of a tale from history or legend. They heard all sorts of things about dragons and wars and Samson and David and Moses and prophets and ill-behaved gods and men and women who weren't scared of them. But after awhile, on one particular night when my brain felt like a pre-squeezed lime slice, I decided that I wanted my spawn to be more active than passive, more invested in the stories. And so, as they gathered around, I told them they could each pick one character (or thing) and I would weave them all into a single story. The arrangement would (I thought) stimulate growth in everyone involved. They got to participate, and I got a creative writing exercise (along with a running start).

And then they discovered hyphens. It was Lucia (then four) who introduced them to our little story sessions. Much to her older brother's chagrin, she loved butterflies. But she didn't love them exclusively. She loved unicorns (especially if they were part butterfly) and ballerinas (especially if they could turn into unicorns and butterflies) and princesses (so long as they knew ballet and could turn into unicorns and butterflies). Ameera (three) added slightly more courageous elements (puppies that could turn into nice girl dragons or clone themselves into whole packs of puppies that could turn into nice girl dragons). What could a brother do but play the game? Rory (five) struggled to counteract all the butterfly-unicorn-ballerina-princessness with more and more gruesome monsters, hoping that his father would take the hint and allow the girlier elements in the story to be devoured—something I was simply unable to do (given that I wanted my daughters sleeping happily).

Things collapsed around my ears. Yeah, I achieved my goals. My kids were involved, and I got help (and a little extra work on my narrative agility). But they weren't supposed to be feeding themselves. And when they tried, it all turned into instant home-brewed irritation.

Rory introduced the giant, creeping land squid that only eats butterfly-unicorn-ballerina-princesses and puppies and girl dragons and can smell them anywhere and can't die and can magically transport itself after its prey and is always really, really hungry. Seamus (one) deeply approved of this monster and displayed his approval with loud roaring. The sisters baulked at such a creature's presence in any narrative ever, let alone their bedtime story. And then Rory profoundly disagreed with my authorial judgment that such a creature must be (somehow) vanquished.

That night, no one went to bed happy, and I knew that I was done shirking. It was time to reshoulder the burden until their instincts had been better fed (and for longer).

ℯↄ

Stories are as hard to create as they are inevitable; good ones are as elusive as they are necessary to hungry souls.

I remember the first time I really felt narrative strain, although I have no idea where I was sitting at the time. The strain (which I just mentioned and which I remember) was going on inside my head. And in the fingers gripping my restless pencil, and in my other fingers smudging what had already been written.

I was going to be a writer. That much I had already proclaimed confidently at the dinner table while in the sixth grade. Which, at that age, made it seem to me like an all-the-way-bank-on-it certainty. After all, I simultaneously loved stories while being incredibly picky. A book gone the least bit wrong was never passable. If I'd been a teacher, anything below a 92% would have been chucked. One little fly in the soup, and there could be no sipping around it. Not only that, but I threw out the pot.

To this day, my wife is surprised at my ability to toss a book across the room fifty pages from the end (and never pick it up again). Rightly or wrongly, the dust from my narrative sandals doth shake off easily.

One problem. My sixth-grade self was spectacular when it came to carping. When it came to flinging an insult off the upper slopes of a curling lip, I played for the varsity squad. But when it came to pointing at my sure-to-be-creating future self and predicting success, I kept it all very . . . *then* and *when I* and *someday*. Never *now*.

But I had (have) a father who was (is) a loather of talk without action, a despiser of tasks undone, a radical perfectionist only bothered by one imperfection—that of not doing. The kind of father who started schools in basements and colleges around dining room tables and churches in auto body shops and publishing houses in bedrooms (decades before the digital revolution).

My father was thrilled that I was going to be a writer. He took me at my word, offering only excitement and congratulations and . . . pressure. Looking back, there was more than a little cunning involved. He called my bluff. But he called it in the hopes that in doing so, the bluff would go away and the writing would be left behind.

Like so many others, I would have been content to assert my aspiration and then piddle away my time without ever pursuing it. Instead, I found myself gripping a pencil. All my previous authorial training had consisted of being a tough crowd and versatile daydreamer. But here I was, tip-toeing into middle school, expected to create art. With words. Because of a few. That had come out of my mouth.

My jolly father was eager to hear my first short story.

One of many strange (and scary) aspects of creating fiction is the physical absorption of the process (when done correctly). A scene is created in the mind. Half of the art is done inside this round bone we keep up on top of our flesh stacks. Things must be conjured up and truly seen. The other half is in getting it out of one's own head and into words that carry it out into the world and attempt to get into the bones of others. An experience is created, captured, given, and hopefully received. The gift is always one of vicarious experience. And getting that experience made is not a tidy process. The words reshape what exists in the mind. The scene in the mind bullies and dodges the words. The imagination grows smoky and fluid and won't sit still, or words simply fail to capture it. One can imaginatively experience all sorts of profound things and still fall absolutely flat when it comes time to paint those things with words.

A critic told me recently that she remembered scenes from one of my newer adventure novels (*The Dragon's Tooth*) not as scenes from a book, but more like personal memories from her own experiences. She couldn't have made me happier. Fiction loves to thwart the filing systems of the mind. (And the mind loves to be thwarted.)

Which is to say, when looking back at my memories of that first work of very juvi fiction, my mind serves up a jumble. I remember a cold cave. I remember heat on one side of me from the fire in the center of that cave along with physical exhaustion and wounded-in-Scottish-battleness. Can you see where things went wrong? As an author, I stood in that imagined cave like the ghost of my main character (who happened to be lying on a cot). I even remember where I was standing as I looked around and examined the uneven stone walls and felt the flame and watched the unwounded men hunching on stools (which they had inexplicably brought along).

But the exhaustion of that character, the woundedness

of that character—those things were just ideas, and ideas are where stories break down. Even good ideas still need incarnation. I didn't feel that character's wound or that exhaustion, and so I remember them as nothing more than a pair of assertions. And the character in that imagined moment was no more than a paper doll as a result. *Now* me shakes my head at *then* me and attempts to shout upriver through Time. Flesh. It. Out.

All ideas must put flesh on if they are to live well (or at least honestly) within a story (any story).

And life is a story.

Atheism is an idea. Most often (thank God), it is an idea lived and told with blunt jumbo-crayon clumsiness. Some child of Christianity or Judaism dons an unbelieving Zorro costume and preens about the living room.

Behold, a dangerous thinker of thinks! A believer in free-from-any-and-all-godness! Fear my brainy blade!

Put candy in their bucket. Act scared. Don't tell them that they're adorable. Atheism is not an idea we want *fleshed out.*

Atheism incarnate does happen in this reality narrative. But it doesn't rant about Islam's treatment of women as did the (often courageous) atheist Christopher Hitchens. It doesn't thunder words like *evil* and mean it (as Hitch so often did) when talking about oppressive communist regimes. His costume slipped all the time—and in many of his best moments.

Atheism incarnate is nihilism from follicle to toenail. It is morality merely as evolved herd survival instinct (non-binding, of course, and as easy for us to outgrow as our feathers were). When Hitchens thundered, he stood in the boots of forefathers who knew that all thunder comes from on high.

But this isn't about atheism.

Life is a story.

Christianity is no good at all as an idea. Stop thinking that an asserted proposition is the same thing as faith. It's a start. But it can also be a costume. Enflesh it.

And what is Christianity incarnate?

Merry Christmas. Join the wise men and find out. Follow the shepherds. Be blind by the road or hungry in a crowd or terrified in a boat or lame at a pool or dangling through the ceiling or a whore with too much perfume or a thief in a tree (or on a tree) or an adulteress facing execution or a liar or a sodomite or a hypocrite or a traitor or all of the above. Be guilty. Betray and despise all that is true and good and beautiful. Walk past that shocked soldier with the sour sponge on the stick. Stand with Mary at the foot of the cross. And see.

The cross is no idea.

This world is all incarnation. Words made flesh. *Words*. God has seen and God has said. His imagination is bone-shaking and soul-shivering, and He has never groped for words to capture (and be) those things. He imagined galaxies and clogged drains and sharks and harmonies and emotions and running and villains and foes and fungus and that heavy marriage of airs that we call water that can skip rocks and light and wind, that can quench and freeze and baptize. He imagined and felt the ache of a mother's love and the mortal yearning caused by the thrust of time and the speed of a falcon and the fear of a hare and minor chords and the smell of carpet glue. And none of these things were any good as ideas. They became words. Sounds mouthed by the Infinite. Rhythms, verbally enfleshed and shaped by the divine. They were spoken.

Which is just another way of saying, *Life is a story*. But *life is a story* is itself a trendy little bit of idea business. It is passed around like a cigarette between furtive fourteen-year-olds, the smoke puffing in and out like empty speech.

If you think it, live it. If you don't live it, you don't really think it. You are not what you think (or what you think you think). You are not what you say you are. You are what you do. You are Adam, charged to name yourself. But you cannot do it with words made noise—only with words made flesh.

Me: I'm going to be a writer.

My father: Here's your pencil.

Me: Darnit.

I stared at that firelight on the wall of the cave longer than anything else. And I remember the sensation of pleasure as I found the word that would capture it better than any other. Dancing. Dancing firelight. Never been used before. By anyone.

Hey, I was young.

When I had finished, I had a story without true narrative progression in which a wounded man woke after a Scottish battle, in a cave with firelight *dancing* on the walls. Celebrating my success, I then read that story out loud to my sisters, my parents, and my grandparents (James and Elizabeth Wilson).

Sisters: Vaguely supportive (I think).

Parents: Very supportive.

Grandmother: Lovingly supportive of me without comment on the narrative.

Grandfather: Critical. Gruff. Appreciative of the effort, but, "Try again kid." Honest.

I found honesty myself. My work (entering middle school) clearly did not measure up to the work of C. S. Lewis (or Tolkien). And so I walked away from it, sagely planning to come back to writing later, when my writing would be better (without practice).

In high school, my father pushed me again. And when he did, everything came out humor.

Humor is safe. The world is full of it. Laughter is a fantastic reward. And humor can lean a lot more on *idea*.

Finally, college. A summer class. A teacher and mentor banned me from any and all humor. I grew. I walked out on the thin, dangerous ice of my imagination, wandering into places that made me nervous (and even terrified).

There are people who write meaningful things. There

are more who desperately want to be seen as writing meaningful things. I lived in fear of becoming one of the latter. And so I never tried to make up or imagine anything meaningful. Instead, I opened my eyes and looked around. I wanted a scapegoat, and so I focused my writing almost entirely on capturing meaning in the nonfiction all around me. Little scenes. Snatches of narratives. The woman and her hilarious children in the apartment below me. I tried to notice everything, to collect and absorb all that I could.

None of it was terribly intentional. It was far more driven by insecurity, by the discomfort I felt imagining emotion and affection. And so I stole. And I accidentally learned something.

Lewis had said that there is no creativity *de novo* in us—that we are all sub-creators pirating and rearranging portions of reality. I agreed. But it was only an idea. And then it took on flesh. I began to see the world more like a cook than a writer. There were boundless ingredients out there, combinations waiting to be discovered and simmered and served. There were truths and stories and characters and quirks that could clash badly, and some that could marry and birth sequels. I began to feel a lot more comfortable. It wasn't all on me to create. It was on me to find. To catch. To arrange.

See. Say.

Some meals involve more layers of discovery—a cow still on the hoof and a reduction sauce with at least seventeen steps. Pizza. Crème brûlée.

Other meals fall into your hand like a heavy pear in autumn. In graduate school, one fell into mine, and suddenly what Lewis had said (and I believed) became real. And I became a writer, not through (as some would say) a discovery of my voice, but through a discovery of my role. Forget the Parisian beret and cigarette. I was a hunter (armed with eyes and a tongue), a cook, a recipient, a mortal among mortals crossing millions of narrative threads every day. I only needed scissors and glue.

All this thanks to a boy (and the One who made him).

The Pitcher

He was there the first time I made the drive. Just off the left side of the road by the stoplight. Winding up and pitching. His motion was jerky and hard, too hard to be accurate. But then he couldn't be more than four years old, and his hand was empty. As I sat at the light I watched the repetition of this exertion. He was off by himself in the grass behind a Lutheran church. There were other children dancing around and stomping, yelling, singing, and falling down. But none of them even noticed the small, black pitcher off to the side, and he never took any notice of them. Then the light changed.

The pitcher stayed in my head all evening. As I sat and discussed Aristotle and Aquinas, his motion repeated itself again and again in my mind. The intensity of his contorted face as each strike blew by a batter, the rapid motion of his small dark arm as he followed through, almost over-balancing, his windup as he slowly stepped back before exploding forward bringing his empty hand around to deliver; all of these things played out on the table in front of me. With a small motion of my fingers I joined in. My pen was swinging at every pitch, hitting nothing but air, strikeout after strikeout. Dust rose off the catcher's glove behind me as each pitch hit its target. Class ended and I went home to eat, my defeat forgotten.

I drove to class four times a week. Four times a week I pulled up to a red light and looked left. Four times a week I watched a small black boy pitch with his heart. He pitched in every scenario. He came from behind, he battled to the wire, and he strolled in victory. I watched him walk around the mound with pride in his step and such a grin on his face that I knew his opposition couldn't be smiling. When he walked and laughed I couldn't help but smile myself. The game was obviously in hand.

But there were other games.

I had run out my door into the usual moist August heat of Maryland without a thought of the pitcher. The world was a grand place even in its humid glory. The wet, warm greens held hands with the dry, stark blues and a breeze blended them both. It wasn't a long drive and I spent most of it looking around at the world. Then, I turned a corner. As was frequently the case, when I saw the light in the distance

I remembered the pitcher. I knew that soon I would look over my shoulder and watch a child swing his empty hand. I would see a small boy off by himself, apart from the games of the others, dreaming. I knew that he would be standing where he always stood, where he could be by himself but still under the eyes of the tired woman from the Lutheran church whose job it was to tend the children born of other women. I knew a pair of small eyes would be staring into nothing and that they would see a batter to defeat and the catcher's target held waiting. He would focus his mind and body beyond the abilities of any of the great pitchers. He would throw with concentration unequaled, because he had no glove on his hand, no hat on his head, no ball in his fist; and while the traffic of Route 70 poured by he could climb the mound, remove reality, and swing his arm.

I didn't look over until I had stopped at the light. And when I did he wasn't pitching; he was circling the mound. By his look I knew he was in a battle. His face registered blank intensity as he walked. There was no pride in it. He strolled to the spot where I knew his eyes saw a dirt mound instead of green grass and he assumed a position that obviously wasn't a windup. He was in the stretch. There were runners on. He glanced right. Runner on third. He glanced left. Runner on first.

"He's going," I tell the inside of my truck, and I can see my pitcher knows. He glances left again. The runner on first starts toward second. The pitch comes, batter takes the strike. Runner on third dances, daring the catcher to throw to second. Runner on first advances. The ball is back on the mound. I glance up at the light. The red glow still hangs in the air, and traffic still streams past.

The pitcher is back in the windup. Runners on third and second. By his face I know we are in the ninth, hopefully the top, but because of the obvious pressure on the pitcher's face I doubt it. His small body stands on the mound gazing at the catcher. He takes a sign and I know it's a fastball.

"Bunt," I whisper. The windup comes, the explosion in the small arm. The light turns, but not before I see the surprise on the pitcher's face. He spins around looking up. He shakes off the glove that only he and I can see and put his hands to his head and stares out to the wall, waiting. The batter took it for a ride. Parked it. Home run, three runs scored. My pitcher falls to the ground in shock. I turn with the traffic and the image is growing smaller in my mirror. A small body in the green grass, the other children don't even look over, but there is a tired woman walking toward it.

After that, I couldn't look at him the same way. The next day he was smiling and strutting again, but even his enjoyment seemed different to me. I could still laugh when he did, but the joy was double-edged. He was surrounded by traffic, given by his parents to be cared for by another; he had no ball and no batter, and still he enjoyed himself.

I would have bought him a ball, but I knew he wouldn't be allowed to throw it. The one time something had risen in his hand it had been a pine cone, and the tired woman had removed it before a single pitch had been completed. I would have stopped and played with him but people didn't take kindly to strangers approaching day care centers. I would have done a lot of things, but I did none of them. Instead I always went to class and watched him pitch from there, the same way he watched a batter crowd the plate.

Then came the last day. There were many distractions to keep me from remembering my pitcher, but for some reason he still climbed into my head. Everything about him flooded my brain as I loaded my book bag. His bib overalls, his over-sized tennis shoes, his uncut hair, all these things presented themselves, and I did not realize why until I was leaving. It was the last day I would ever see him. It was the last game of the season. I would drive by, watch him throw his arm, and drive on. Only this time driving on was permanent. I would never make the drive again. I would be flying home the next morning. I realized that he was a boy who I had always wanted to talk to; I wanted to know his name and his mind; I wanted to see all of his life. But I was driving by.

The drive felt longer than it usually did and I spent the time not thinking about class, or the past summer session, but about that thin boy with an empty hand. I wondered about his father, and if he had played baseball. I wondered if he had simply seen it on TV and latched on to it. His behavior was detailed enough in its imitation that he had to have watched a good deal of baseball. I thought about his drive. His desire to pitch as hard as he could when he wasn't throwing anything to anybody and knew it. But I knew he went home tired every night. Tired from the workout of throwing his arm. Where did his love of the game come from? Where was his father? Who would play catch with him? We were all too busy. We were driving by. His father and mother were driving by. I was driving by. A thousand others were driving by. Only the tired woman wasn't driving by, and she was busy, busy sitting and making sure my pitcher didn't really throw anything. He was as invisible to the world as his catcher and the batters he struck out. Humanity's traffic sped by him and had stored him safely on a piece of grass that he had made into a mound. All things were blind to him, and he returned the favor.

I reached his street and looked at the light hanging in the distance. It was green. It was never green. It would change. I kept driving and watching the light. It wasn't changing. I began to feel nervous. I needed to say good-bye to the pitcher. I looked for a place to pull over but there was nothing. I was in the left lane with traffic on my right and oncoming. I was through the light, and I had only enough time to glance over my shoulder as I turned.

The pitcher was standing on his mound staring into nowhere. He wasn't pitching. Was he taking a sign? I couldn't tell. I grabbed my mirror and saw the beginning of a windup before he disappeared.

The next semester I had moved and didn't need to make that drive anymore. But I did. I drove by before class. The grass was empty of everything. There were no children laughing and screaming and falling down. There was no tired woman. There was no pitcher. I drove to class. I sat at the table. Someone was talking about Homer. I looked down. My pen was swinging.

More than a decade later, I can still see him. I hope that he is somewhere with real cleats and real leather and a real ball in his hand.

In some ways, he taught me how to catch (even if clumsily).

e

These days, the youngest of my offspring gets the most verbal storytelling. For the others (and for her, eventually), I have written novels, stories about cousins chipping plaster off of walls to discover magic cupboards and journeys through worlds, stories about siblings swept up in an ancient order of explorers, and one about a boy sucked down into a cave on a makeshift raft. And I sit my kids down and float them new stories, gauging their reactions.

I have diced reality, simmered and sautéed, baked and barbecued, and served up the best soul food that I can. I'm still in the kitchen. I hope to die in the kitchen.

Life is a story. We are all characters. Characters need food and characters need grooming.

I am often asked why I write fiction for children. Because those whom I am called to feed are still children. Because I am still a child. Because the world is big, and the world is wonderful, but it is also terrifying. It is an ocean full of paper boats. And for many children, the only nobility, the only joy, the only strength and sacrifice that they see first-hand—that they see enfleshed—comes in fiction. Imagined friends and heroes can shape loves and loyalties and choices as much (or more) as real ones. Even when children have plenty of joy in their lives, good stories reinforce it. And I write for children because I have read more than my fair share of adult ideas set out and explained by adult think-ers and theologians, philosophers and pundits, and I may as well admit that I have been more influenced (as a person) by my childhood readings of Tolkien and Lewis, and by those moments listening to tales of Tiny Tim, and by that stack of pages my father handed me about an imaginary goblin war, than by any idea books that I read in college and grad school. The events and characters in Narnia and Middle Earth shaped my ideals, my dreams, my loyalties, and my goals. Kant just annoyed me.

Stories are the closest our own words can ever come to being made flesh—gifts unwrapped in the imagination.

Even now that my children can inhale adventures hun-dreds of pages long, they are thrilled when the word goes out that an oral story is coming. It tends to happen around birthdays and holidays and weeks spent at the beach.

The main characters are always the same. And the series title is simple but accurate: The Wilson Kid Adventures.

You see, there was this old man, and a magpie had stolen

his two magic stones, and as he was chasing that bird he ran into four (now five) children. Their names were Rory, Lucia, Ameera, Seamus, and Marisol, and little did they know what catching that magpie would mean.

No more butterfly-unicorn-ballerina-princesses. No more giant, creeping land squids or self-cloning puppies. But there is a palace in the sky and a friendly dragon and a personable elephant and a young (and very soft) tiger and a flying stick and a Peruvian mine full of magical treasures and a great pyramid that turned out to be just the tip of an enormous buried obelisk.

And that should be enough for anyone.

THREE

Eyes Back: 1

UNWIND THE PLANETS. DROP THE YO-YO AND LET IT hum, unspooling seven looping decades. All of my grand-parents were alive. The story of this world was grinding pain and chewing gravel, while I was tucked away safely in the future's distant womb. Hop around the spherical ball of story—pick out four threads.

Elizabeth Catherine Dodds was a tough young Canadian woman. Her family had been shattered by both hardship and the treatment of that hardship with alcohol. Parents were gone. Brothers were at war (and would both be killed). As a teenage girl, she had been informally fostered by another family. Eventually, the matriarch had announced that things had gotten altogether too sloppy around the edges, and had ordered everyone off to a tent meeting. Elizabeth "Bessie" Dodds was given faith in a tent.

In Casper, Wyoming, Margaret Downing was singing silly sorority songs surrounded by girls more frustrated by what the war was doing to their social lives than by any real sense of the danger swallowing the Far East and Europe. Margaret was being courted by a man I have heard nothing much about—he gave her a ring, but he was no near relative of mine.

Not too far outside Omaha, Nebraska, a fifteen year-old boy named James Irwin Wilson was facing the toughest challenge of his young life. He was big. His older brother had been sent to war, and he was left behind to work the small farm and the many odd jobs his father juggled to keep the clan alive. James was the family muscle. His father took him into town to plow victory gardens for small pay. Together they hitched a plow to a big black draft stallion and a much smaller mare, to help set a slower pace. When the mare grew sick, James watched his father unhitch her and then wage a farmer's war with the stallion to turn the soil. Then he watched him war with the landowner about fair pay. Then, with the mare and the stallion hitched to a wagon on the road home, he watched the mare collapse and the stallion rear, and his father jump to unhitch them both. As the stallion thundered away, James watched his father collapse with a heart attack. At fifteen, with the tenth grade to finish, his older brother at war (on a doomed destroyer), a younger brother with polio, his father flat on his back, the outhouse overflowing, and everything on that ten-acre farm pregnant—including his mother—James Irwin Wilson began to become himself.

Scroll around the globe and down. At that same time, in the South Pacific, Lawrence Aubry Greensides is caught in the battle of Guadalcanal. The tall, hard-driven, laughing, overachieving bomber co-pilot was out painting fake craters on the tarmac when the air raid began, and he hopped onto an overloaded passing Jeep before the bombs began to fall. With his feet on the fender and his rear on the hood, he was the ornament for that Jeep when it drove into the impact of a Japanese bomb.

Clearly, I was not meant to be.

Going to Hell in a Seventeen-Passenger Handbasket: Stories Lived

WE'D MANAGED TO ROCKET OVER THE NORTH POLE without incident. Our wings hadn't fallen off. The kids had been cheerful, excited, fed, exhausted, and asleep. Nine hours to leap from Seattle, stripe the night sky above worlds of ice, and then drop down toward isles that once held approximately 87.5 percent of my modern ancestors and that now held my sister, my brother-in-law, their five children, and our waiting adventure.

Just a few days before, I had called my sister and had asked her a simple question: If we fly over on Thursday, would you guys feel like renting a van, picking us up in London, and then road-tripping to Rome and back up again?

She hadn't even needed to call me back. The cousins were in.

Rome (and everything between London and Rome) was a little bit exciting for the eldest of our young people. But being with the cousins? In a van? For days and days?

Jubilation. Ecstasy.

Seamus was the wild card. He was two at the time and went by a simpler nickname: Fatty.

"How do you think Fatty will do?" my wife asked (herself as much as me).

There was only one way to find out.

Retrospectively, we called the trip EUROCOUSINTOUR 2009. Other names could have worked, but they all grew too narrow or too broad and unwieldy.

FATTY SAD ALL OVER just misses so much of the joy. And he wasn't sad all over. Just most places.

The drama started in the Jetway. We landed. I woke the children. I picked up Fatty and he buried his face in my neck. The other kids slipped on their new backpacks and their excitement began to slowly climb up through their weariness, sparkling in their sleep-fogged eyes. We were near the front of the plane and made our way easily down the aisle, smiled at the flight attendants, received their compliments on the perfection of our brood, and then began our ascent up the Jetway.

Something hot and heavy slapped into my neck and ran down my back. I paused and looked around. I lifted Fatty up. He hit me with another hot chuck from the front.

Just behind me, Rory panicked at the sight. He spread his legs, fully blocking all the passenger traffic behind us and sympathy-puked on the floor.

My wife reached for Fatty.

No. We had to get out of this tube before anything else could be addressed. She grabbed the girls, I grabbed Rory, and we all began to accelerate. But Fatty wasn't done. He painted on. And every time he did, Rory slipped my grip and stopped, hands on knees, corking dozens of people in behind him.

No. Rory. No.

Yes. Daddy. Yes.

Fatty's depths were unplumbed. Holding one human fountain and dragging another, I commanded Rory not to watch his brother. It didn't matter. My oldest son polka-dotted that Jetway with pizza (imported from Seattle) at least every ten feet.

And I began to laugh. Hard. And very, very alone.

My wife and the girls were out. The crowd behind us diligently admired abstract space with glassy eyes. Dozens of business-traveling Brits attempted to erase us from existence with flat faces, but their Jedi tricks couldn't touch our hard reality.

We Wilson boys were there with flesh on, and we were

hilarious. Two of us were throwing up. One of us was wheezing laughter beneath the spatter.

That sweet and holy concourse greeted us with wider spaces and freer air and our wide-eyed female counterparts. My wife's laughter joined my own, but tinted with more grimace and horror.

Dozens and dozens of people flowed past us in a river, missing this gift, this slapstick punch line to a long flight, offered to them by a whimsical God.

Thanks to the infinite bureaucratic wisdom of some tom-fool security consultant (or appointed official), Heathrow had determined that rubbish bins were a security hazard. And so there were none.

Heather began to strip Fatty. I stripped off my soggy sweater. I gathered up our shed garments like the righteousness of twin Pharisees and then threw the heavy wad enthusiastically against the wall. It slapped and sank.

Where there be no rubbish bin, all is rubbish bin.

And so our adventure began.

Lesson 1: When one begins to make claims about life and its storyness, one should be careful. Stories tend to follow, and stories involve unpleasantness. God calls bluffs, and makes narrative hypocrites of us all.

Lesson 2: When faced with unpleasantness (trouble) there are only two ultimate responses (with many variations). On the one hand, "The Lord gives, the Lord takes away, blessed be the name of the Lord." On the other, "Curse God and die."

Variations on the latter can include whining, moping, self-pity, apathy, or rage. Variations of the former can include laughter, song, retellings, and an energetic attack of obstacles.

If God gives you (or makes you) a joke, what are you meant to do in response? (Receive it. Laugh.)

If God gives you an obstacle, what are you meant to do in response? (Receive it. Climb it. Then laugh.)

If God gives you more profound hardship, what are you meant to do in response? (Receive it. Climb it. Then laugh. Exhibit A: His Son.)

Fatty made it into an umbrella stroller wearing only a pull-up. I was wearing a mostly damp undershirt (but figured the Brits would prefer it to my skin). Thanks to Rory's wide-stance-hunch technique, he was virtually unscathed.

Eventually we formed a luggage trolly-train, my sister found us, and we were led outside to our communal steed.

Five cousins and an uncle were waiting inside an enormously long, white, bulbous van with a bloated abdomen and a discreet RENT ME label on its hindquarters. Its wheels were awkwardly tiny for its enormous length (and girth), and the whole thing was shaking with internal cousin-caused excitement hidden behind tinted windows.

Naturally, we loaded up and headed for Luxemburg.

e⌒

There is a school of American thought that suggests we are supposed to live furiously and foolishly when young, slave away pointlessly when adults, and then coast into low-impact activity as soon as financially possible.

Isn't that just a kiss on the lips (from a dog).

The truth is that a life well lived is always lived on a rising scale of difficulty.

As a little kid, I had a job: Obey my mother. Don't lie. Play hard. Be kind to my sisters.

At the time, that job was actually difficult. My mom kept saying things like, "Come here." And, "No jumping on the couch." Or, "Don't stand on the doorknob and swing on the door." And, "No hitting."

But my sisters were there, and so were my fists. The couch was bouncy. Doors are cool to swing on.

Man, I was bad at my job.

I remember the existential despair as I stood in the front yard of our duplex with my real yellow fiberglass bow with a real arrow on the string, but on that arrow's tip . . . a tube sock with red stripes duct-taped on tight.

I still managed to shoot it over the fence.

I remember kneeling on my top bunk and pounding nails into my wall in a long, winding row that even crossed my Seattle Seahawks poster.

Throughout my childhood, the second most common (bad) sound effect was most likely glass shattering, only occurring slightly less frequently than the yelping of a sister.

But I was supposed to push the limits. That was my job at the time. I was supposed to live as fully as I could within the boundaries of the law. I transgressed often, but a balance between full-throttle living and obedience was found with much help from wooden kitchen spoons.

I learned how a raw egg reacts beneath a hammer and how far I could throw a hatchet. Sure, I mounded toilet paper up in the toilet bowl and then lit it on fire, but at least I flushed.

And just as I began to get good at my job, I got promoted. The law remained the same, but the number of ways in which it was possible to transgress radically increased. I was bigger. I was faster. I was at school.

It's that way for all of us. But the promotions come regardless of whether or not we've actually improved. If you are bad at being two, you will be bad at being four. If you're bad at being four, you will be bad at being six.

Temptations increase. Potential falls multiply. We look at a two-year-old attempting to overthrow righteousness and establish evil in all the land, and we snicker. Lazy parents tell themselves that the wee little he (or she) will outgrow this little tendency of theirs.

Yipes. Wong. Buzzer. Gong.

What they mean is that the child will grow into someone else's problem. Once they are at day care, the struggle will be out of sight and will be dealt with by other struggling peers and/or unrelated adults. Or not.

The school years escalate in difficulty and multiply in temptation. Add sports and friends and hormones and petty power structures. You can now sit in huge chunks of hurtling metal, taking the lives of every one of your passengers and every passenger in every other passing chunk of metal and every passing pedestrian and every passing bicyclist into your irresponsible hands. You can now make mistakes that kill people (and you). Off to college and mustachioed professors will pour nonsense all over you. You are ready or you aren't. Peers wallow in every kind of debauch. You are ready or you aren't. And you can now (far more easily than in high school) ruin your life forever.

You are now on your own.

And then you aren't. Other real live souls are now depending on you. You are the creator of their childhoods. You are the influencer of their dreams and tastes and fears. You are the emcee of all reality, the one to introduce those small people to the true personality of their Maker (as imaged by your life more than your words). The choices you now make have lives riding on them. Always. Their problems and struggles are yours to help them resolve. Their weaknesses yours to strengthen. Or not. (Maybe they'll outgrow them.)

This X marks my spot. I am here. For good and ill, I am a molder of childhoods, an instiller of instincts, a feeder (or famisher) of souls, a sensei of humor. I am an image of God (stunted and vandalized but all the earthly father my kids can have). Thank God for faith and bulk-ordered grace.

As the next decades flicker past, my burden will change.

I will begin to ride my bike with no hands, watching my children be what they will be. I will reap what has been sown. I will see the fruit of faith (and the fruit of failures). And I will see my children sow again, but on their own.

I will labor to live with the joyful fury of a child, but I will be exhausted. My body will decay and break. That part has already begun. I will grow weak, but with the memory of strength, reaching for strength that should be there and is now gone.

In the end, I will face the greatest enemy that any man has ever faced. And I will lose.

Our challenges always build. A ninety-five-year-old man sits in his chair with a wandering mind because a century cannot pass without many blows. That much life is heavy for the strongest shoulders. A young man might feel bold; he might feel courageous, gambling with life and death. And he might be courageous. But he trusts his strength; he feels as if he could fight, as if he could run, as if he has a chance. He may even choose his danger.

It takes a different kind of courage to face death when you cannot run, when you cannot fight, when you are pinned beneath heavy decades, beneath the weight of life— when your faith really must be in another.

I spoke with Lawrence Greensides—Granddad—often. But not often enough. He was a man with big shoulders and a strong back, carrying nearly a century before the weight finally dropped him to his knees.

He was my expert whenever some adventure story required knowledge of planes. He was a man who faced bullets and bombs and storms, who was willing to end his life story in the service of his country, his family, his men. And he came close. But even after two wars, the heaviest burden he ever carried was still at the end in a quiet house where his wife sat in a swing that he had hung for her, watching the birds. Because at the end, he carried all of it. Ninety-five years of fallen choices. Of mistakes. Of darkness. Of frustrations. Of regrets. Ninety-five years of life means ninety-five years of loss.

He felt that weight as he cared for his sweet and forgetful wife. He would try to pick up his faults, his memory wandering over old scars. It was crushing. And then relief would come and he would laugh as happily as the day I saw him baptized. He didn't have to carry the weight. It wasn't his anymore. It had all been taken and hung on a tree. It had been bound to a broken body with strips of cloth and buried, and it was still in that grave, left there on one bright Sunday morning long ago when Life, this story, turned.

I had called him not long before when my mother warned me that something was changing. He was having dizzy spells. Abdominal pain.

I made a mental note to call him again. But I didn't. If I am blessed to live to his length, a day will come in 2073 when I am sitting beneath the burden of a century, and my mind's finger will trace the scar of this regret. By then, it will be soon healed.

My grandmother was on her swing when my uncle found his father on his knees. He tried to help him up, but my grandfather was focused on his last fight.

"No," he said. "I'm dying."

And he did.

Someday I will face death. I'm building up to it. For now, I face carpool. And deadlines. And book tours. And some back pain. And the task of molding childhoods. And occasional vomit.

℮

The Fatty threw up in France. He threw up in Belgium. We pitied the child's discovery of motion sickness at the early age of two, but we plowed on (my hands never far from a plastic bag). Eventually he settled into sleep, but even then his young face with pinched brows was a picture of self-pity, of one persecuted by his parents.

In Luxemburg we discovered just how large we were living. Nine children? From just two couples? The wealthy semi-Germans gaped at us like we were pulling these kids from the ears of strangers in some sort of unrequested magic trick. And a rude, vulgar, and distasteful magic trick it was too. Even in the Luxemburgan McDonald's (where club music was throbbing and the meals weren't happy), we faced the curling of thin European lips.

The man at the hotel didn't care what he had said on the phone. He didn't care what we had reserved. He absolutely and under no circumstances could allow families like ours to parade freely around the premises. I think we needed special licenses.

(We had warned the kids that they might be meeting some rude resistance to their existence, and they behaved like good little marines even as the hotel manager did his best impression of the Child Catcher from *Chitty Chitty Bang Bang*.)

Okay, fine. We could stay. But only if the small children stayed in their own room on a separate floor. Whatever, Heinrich. We placated the villain of this piece by paying for rooms we wouldn't use and acting like we would happily send wee children off on their own.

At breakfast we got our own back. We entered the hotel restaurant like a gypsy caravan. Children were such a scarcity that when one or two did grace the establishment, they were entitled to receive a free stuffed moose.

The mooses just kept coming. A stunned hostess even hustled off to a storage closet and returned with more. We ate up the moose quota deep into the next year.

Diners stopped dining. Waiters stopped waiting. We let the nine children sit by themselves and told them to shock the world with their perfect behavior.

And they did.

Look, Heinrich, no hands. Four wise and savvy parents

sat at their own table and observed the effect of their children with wry amusement. You would have thought we'd left nine white tigers on those stools cheerfully sipping cream tea.

Pride, as the man said, goeth.

Without thorough and cautious adult supervision, Fatty ate nine sausages and then, as a moment of silent peace spread throughout the room, threw them back up on the floor.

We fled quickly, clutching our mooses.

In Heidelberg, I smuggled all nine children up an elevator before hotel staff could take note. The next morning, Fatty threw up on his plate. My sister disappeared the evidence, and the event went unnoticed by our fellow diners. We were becoming professional covert up-chuckers.

Chinese tourists asked to be photographed with our band of small people. At first it was funny, but these were men and women who had lived beneath hard laws of Molech—abortion by law. Limit: one soul from every two. To those smiling people with the cameras, we were wealthy beyond measure, inhabitants of heaven on earth. They weren't wrong.

Early Sunday morning, we followed the church bells through old cobbled Heidelberg toward worship. We were late. And embarrassed. It was going to be awkward enough already, strolling in with our hordes (without any intention of banishing them to non-English-speaking Sunday school with non-English-speaking strangers). But now we were going to make a full-on scene with our tardiness.

The church was huge, centered in an old European square where empty market stalls lined its sides. Late already, we walked to the wrong end, a full city block away from the entrance.

Hey, back home, our church meets in a gym.

The men who preached here wrote the *Heidelberg Catechism*, which we still use weekly. They were anchors in the shield wall of the Reformation. We wanted to dip our feet in that history.

And then I heard the rattle of two bicycles. A young blond woman was frantically—and guiltily—pedaling toward us. A young dark-haired lad pedaled beside her. They were both disheveled, and wearing the clear look of recent nookie participants . . . along with their black robes.

They leapt off their bicycles, locked them up while furtively whispering to each other, unlocked a side door, and snuck inside.

We rounded the church and entered through the main doors, expecting that those two might be delinquent choir members.

He did the Scripture reading. She did the preaching.

Clearly, the Reformation had moved on. We left in search of a Starbucks.

In northern Italy, my wife led a hotel concierge up to the cab of the van for a casual chat while I quickly smuggled ducking cousins out of the rear emergency door and into the hotel.

Lawrence Greensides had warned us about Rome, though he had last been through that city in the 1950s.

Watch yourself. It's nothing personal, but those Romans will all look for a pound of flesh. Expect waiters to gouge you on the bill and then grab one of your children to distract you from closer examination. Expect to be given food "on the house" and then be charged for it. Expect someone to try and rob you every time you turn around. Oh, and don't *drink the water.*

Granddad was like that. Mr. Cynic.

We were traveling with eleven bags. In Rome, we reached our gated hotel beside the walls of the Vatican at around 10:00 p.m. By 10:05 p.m., Rome had lightened our load a great deal. From that moment on, we were traveling with two bags.

Hotel staff vanished nine of our bags before we had even managed to check in. And suddenly everyone had wide eyes and no English.

Drama, drama. Accusations. Investigations. We got nowhere. Because we weren't screaming and breaking things. Those Romans watched our body language, our American self-control, and they ignored our words. Clearly, they could push us harder. So they double-charged us for the rooms.

We didn't get anywhere until my wife started yelling at them in Spanish.

The next morning we sent a photo to Granddad . . . of

his great-grandkids pretending to drink the water from a public fountain.

We were told so many things by so many people before this trip.

Oh, you haven't really been to Rome until you eat/drink/walk/stay here/there/everywhichwhere.

Yeah? Well you haven't been to Rome until you drop in with nine kids and only the clothes on your backs. We were visiting the great city more organically, in the historical spirit of medieval pauper pilgrims summoned as prey by the ancient holy stones.

Fatty wasn't throwing up anymore, but he no longer had his jammers (much confused grief), his rubber monster galoshes (many requests), his coat, his pull-ups.

"Kids," I said as we strolled through the Forum, smelling like the buskers. "Have I ever told you about the founding of Rome?"

We talked about thievery, thieves, con men, and gangsters. We talked about Rome's origin and heritage and the grand and classical tradition of taking other people's stuff—money, nations, lives.

Then we climbed down into the cells of the Mamertine Prison. Tiny, wet, and dark. A cold place to wait for death, a grave for the living.

According to stories that trace back at least to the 400s, this is where the apostle Peter was held before he was crucified. This is where the apostle Paul was held before he was beheaded. Two men who had burned with furious light, two foxes who had raced through the vineyard with torches tied to their tails by Christ Himself—that great Samson. In this place they had waited for death, for the finish lines to their races, for the last flurry of blows in their fight—they fought well to the end.

They had reached their deaths by living.

So will we. How much of the vineyard can we burn first? How fast can we run? How deeply can we laugh? Can we ever give more than we receive? How much gratitude can we show? How many of *the least of these* can we touch along the way? How many seeds will we get into the ground before we ourselves are planted?

In those small cells it was hard to care about missing clothes.

Beneath St. Peter's, we walked through the crypts of the popes. Fatty's hand was in mine, and fermented thoughts were stirring.

Up ahead, an icon of St. Peter marked his tomb. But between myself and that box full of apostolic dust, there was a praying crowd. Men and women held back by velvet ropes were crying and whispering prayers and ticking beads under the stern eyes of a middle-aged guard. Fatty and I approached, and I saw the object of this crowd's reverence.

The crypt of John Paul II.

I was confused.

I pray to my omniscient, omnipresent, omnispeaking

Father, and I do it in the name of my triumphant Elder Brother, the Firstborn of Righteousness, Firstborn in the Resurrection, Conqueror of Death.

Though I am crazy to talk this way, if I was going to pray to someone else, I would be more inclined to pray to Christ's close friend, His rock, the foundation of His church. Not to someone who was friends with Bono.

But that's just me.

The stern guard glared at me, and I realized that Fatty had slipped my grip. In his newfound enthusiasm for life, my son ducked a velvet rope and hopped into a row of papal sarcophagi. My heart might have stopped, but my limbs hadn't. I was already jumping the rope after him, as he focused on one marble box, flattened his small hands, and began thumping on its side.

The boy had gone pope slapping.

I grabbed my son's hand and led him back toward the center aisle, grimacing apologetically at the irritated guard as I did. And then I glanced back at the sarcophagus, at the name cut into the marble.

Ah. It was just one of those Renaissance johnnies. My son was kinder than Dante. I found my grip on his hand loosening. He was, after all, so hard to control. Like an Inquisition.

On the return, we got lost in northern Italy, wandering back and forth across the French border in the middle of the night, even paying a toll to a man identical to C. S. Lewis in every way (except that he lied to us).

We visited Carcassonne, castle of cultists, and we awarded France the Yankee Medal for Best Gas Station Food. We shot the Alps in the dark and waved at Lichtenstein as we darted past.

Underwear was purchased at a flea market, no doubt stolen from some other hapless Americans.

We learned that the best gelato in all of Rome was in Heidelberg.

We lived all over. And we pointed our noses home. To Oxford. To London. To Seattle. To Idaho. To bed.

We lost everything but our children and our camera and our stroller.

We gained more.

FIVE

City Hiatus: Rome

HERE I AM, STROLLING DOWN THE POPE'S HALLWAY, staring at the ceiling. I decorate my shoulders with a two-year-old boy and attempt to manage a camera. You should see the footage.

INT. POPE'S HALLWAY - DAY

A family of six moves through an intensely colorful medieval hallway, flowing with the crowd like farm salmon trying to blend in on the spawn.

NARRATOR (OFF SCREEN)
Lucia! Lucy! Lucy! Lu-Lu!

LUCIA, 5, pretty, permanently surprised
eyes, staring at her feet as she walks,
finally looks up.

>   **NARRATOR (O.S.)**
> Say "hi"!

>   **LUCIA**
> Hi.

>   **NARRATOR (O.S.)**
> Where are you?

>   **LUCIA**
>   (scrunching face)
> Italy?

RORY, 7, leaps into the frame.

>   **RORY**
> Rome!

That is correct, Rory. We are in Rome. More specifically,
we are in Vatican City (yadda, yadda, sovereignty, independence, Swiss people with poofy pants and halberds). Even
more specifically, we are in a little place I like to call the
pope's hallway. (If it's not his, then whose is it?)

More specifically still, we are walking through a tunnel of art. I don't know where to put my eyes as we flow
along with the other salmon. These walls and ceilings are
arting at me at a greater painting-per-step ratio than any
walls and ceilings have ever dared attempt before or since.

For sanity's sake, I watch my toes for a few strides—the floor is comparative vanilla—and miss enough paintings to keep every museum in the western United States overstocked with medieval nudes of the well-known and awfully lengthy belly-paunch movement. A few strides more and they could each fill a new wing labeled (for purposes of simplicity) *Unlimited Renaissancey Bible Scenes and Things.* PG-13.

On the traditional art density scale of wine cooler to whiskey, let's just say this place could preserve organs in jars for science class.

So why am I, one exuberantly interested in the arts (pensive expression), now pointing my camera at Ameera (age four, big smile) and determining if she knows where on this planet her parents have currently dragged her? Why am I commanding the young son on my shoulders to stare at the walls while I merely glance at the contents of one-tenth (tops) of these painted-on gilt frames, and instead become deeply distracted by Asian tourists with bigger (and tinier) cameras than mine?

Because I'm a sucker for a time lapse. There's a bigger scene here. There is a frame outside these many, many frames. Is there a brochure for the big picture? Can I peek in on the architects' meeting when they first discussed this place and the Sistine Chapel it leads to? When will this hallway fall down? How many Koreans come here? Who was the first Korean to come here? Will my kids remember this? Hey kids, where are you? Will I remember this? Point the camera at the wall. Oil-based people flashing thigh for attention are doing something or other. Which Bible story is this? Sorry, thigh-flashy people, I'm moving on. When I write about you years from now I won't even remember your faces. I turn the camera, suddenly aware that I will never care about that painting after this moment. Ever. I'm wasting tape. Hey Rory, what do you think? Boy on my shoulders (Seamus), look up. Too bad you forgot your crayons.

In this world, there is no true freeze frame. Pictures do not escape time. But they do sit in it. Pictures are men grabbing at wind to make themselves feel less beaten by the driving current of this river. We pinch brushes to pinch moments, feelings, and . . . that thing that was just now but now it's gone. Did you catch that? We push buttons and point electric boxes. Did you get that? And most of the time we never go back to look. I got it (I think). But we feel better, like fishermen hooking everything but reeling rarely.

In the history of the world, how many men and women have lived? How many moments have been seen? How much yearning drove how many people to paint how many pictures? To carve how many rocks? To snap how many shots?

Question: What percentage of the totality of man's creations through all of time are now in museums?

Answer: Insert made-up number here.

Who cares? Is it a waste to grasp at moments? To try and catch the wind between my forefinger and my thumb?

To feel and see and taste and touch the music of the world, to glimpse the transcendent in the simple and the simple in the transcendent, to shiver with awe at the sight of a child studying foot-pounded dust, while twisting slowly in the air above it, head and shoulders through a tire swing? To stare for an hour at the still, black surface of a lake, to marvel at the invention of water and my need to swallow it, feel it, and ride it?

I stretch my mouth wide with words until my jaw aches, and still I fail. I grab a pencil to sketch and I fail even faster. I stare at the slowly spinning child staring at the earth, and I know that if I reach for my phone, for the appropriate app, and worm forward to catch the appropriate angle, that I will not really capture this thing called *now*. I am only throwing a pebble at the lake, adding my little ripples. But I don't care. I will have participated, I will have joined in the creation, like an ant leaning a leaf against a skyscraper and brushing off his forelegs, glad to have helped.

Can I ever be fed, and need no more food? Can I ever sleep and need no more rest? Can I ever feel my wife beside me as we watch living, eternal, laughing things we were used to create, and not want to see them again tomorrow? Can I ever stop my mouth from trying to harness the world with mere noises made by my flesh-bellows buzzing flesh-strings with puffs of air that echo in my nose?

When God stops, I will. My rumblings and ramblings are a vibration within His own.

I stand before you now, a picture. You sit or stroll or recline, a picture.

The Koreans in the pope's hallway turn from thick Adam and lumpy Eve to observe the large, loud American, his four children, and his wife. They think thoughts. They draw conclusions. What is the story they see?

I am museum exhibit number however-many-people-you-have-ever-seen-in-your-life.

I was made. I am a picture of God (*imago dei*). Of His Son (grafted into the New Adam). I am a hangnail in the larger picture of His Son's bride, the church. (I live in Idaho; a hangnail is generous.)

We grasp because God does. We create, and fall short, because God does. We continue creating because we fell short, and fall short again, because God does. Because one act of creation, one attempt at capture, is only one breath and we must breathe again. And again. And again. Here we stand (and sit and sleep), the many images of the Imager, and we can do no other.

The throat tightens. Nervousness builds. Orthodox hackles rise (rightly).

God? Fall short? Yes. But only in a frozen frame.

Breathe with me now. Stick close. You are made in the image of God. Check. (Long pause.) Have you seen yourself lately? Because I've seen myself, and it's not like I see a resemblance to the Infinite Creator God. There are moles on my soul. Hairy ones. Jeepers, let's keep that rib cage closed, please, shall we? Also, my nose is crooked. *But other than that . . .*

Ha.

God—the God who bowled the fire in the sky, who spun the moon and flung the stars, who parted the waters, who feathered birds and scaled fish and furred bears, who called up trees, who invented fruit and bats and oceans and wind and lightning and gave Jupiter a red cowlick for an eye— that God challenged Himself. He made a pile of dust on the ground in a garden and He decided to make a picture of Himself.

He fell short. (In a frozen frame.)

In the pope's hallway, I peek behind a trash can. There is a painting behind it. I want to say it was of Enoch, but that is more likely false than true.

In the 1950s, when Lawrence Greensides came to this place, he dragged along his son, Robert, his daughter, Marla, and his lovely wife, Margaret. He also brought an 8mm camera to suck in moments so that later he could coil them, stick them on a machine, and spray light through them through a crystal lens, and onto a little screen he pulled from the closet in his home in Coeur d'Alene, Idaho, while I (and my two sisters) patiently ate colored marshmallows on the carpet.

"Oh, will you look at that," my grandmother says from her chair behind us. Her voice is sweetness itself, part apple pie and part clean laundry left to ride the wind in the sun. Always has been.

There she is, on the screen, young and fresh. Small Aunt Marla and little Uncle Bob stand beside her. An American family takes in the Vatican. They smile and wave jerkily.

```
EXT. VATICAN CITY - DAY
The camera pans off of an American family
and climbs the buildings, passing windows
and roofs.
                              CUT TO:

EXT. VATICAN ROOF - DAY
The same camera now looks down on the
square, on all the tourists. It turns
and BOB, on the roof with the cameraman,
waves. The camera pans further up,
passing windows and resting on the top.
                              CUT TO:

EXT. UPPER VATICAN ROOF - DAY
The same camera is now all the way on
the roof with Bob. The edge is lined
with statues. The middle is peaked. Shots
down at the square. Zoom in on the pope's
personal apartment window. Shots as a
GUARD (black uniform, helmet) approaches
to remove the cameraman and Bob.
```

I have that camera. But more importantly, I have another camera. Last summer, I set my camera up in my grandfather's house. I cast a feeble net, trying to catch a life, a man of two wars and four children, a man of wounds and faith and adventures. I went grasping for wind, and I caught two handfuls. This summer, I handed that camera to my son while I stood beside a box wrapped with a flag, and I choked out words too small.

I am more than a painting, because I do not sit in time. I am a failed portrait of God, but this is no frozen frame. He hasn't finished. And He never will. He cannot fall short, because He will never stop His mouth.

We are dust. We are the challenge of the dust. Mix dust with breath. Picture God.

The pope's hallway is behind us. We enter the Sistine Chapel. The ceiling is, indeed, there. It is, indeed, painted. But the greater art crowds beneath it. We all crane our necks, staring straight up at the work of one man imprisoned by a pope until he had finished. Sour, cynical men in uniforms shush every whisper with a wet enthusiasm, proving they don't really care about noise. People. Hundreds of us. From dust. The kind of people who whisper and shush and paint ceilings and make other people paint ceilings. The kind of people who sit on their Father's shoulders and wonder what's going on and when it will stop. Korean people attempting to hip-shoot photos when the shush guards aren't looking, and the well-trained shush guards who catch them.

In Hell's Canyon, there are rough stone carvings thousands of years old. In one image, a stick man falls from a dotted line cliff to his doom.

Thousands of years ago, one man watched another man chip at a rock, thinking of their fallen mutual friend. Perhaps a brother. They strain to remember. To capture. To anchor some moment against the roiling river of time.

"Did you get it?" the observer asks. The artist shrugs, frustrated.

SIX

Born to Trouble

I STAND IN QUIET HEAT, BESIDE MY CAR IN A PARKED line of cars behind a hearse. We are on a high, wide field half a mile above the level of the sea, with sloping green shoulders stretched out beneath a low, wide sky. My grandfather did not want to go into the ground with pomp and military formality, but God does as He wills when He wills. I'm not even wearing a tie, but the day arrived in its dress blues, as bright and sharp and formal as any day could be. The sky is a deep, well-brushed blue, the sun's gold has been polished bright, and long blades of gleam mark it with a rigid cross too bright for eyes. Beneath it all, the grass is green enough to be Irish, and cropped tight enough to be military. But there is only a small gathering of stones.

This cemetery is young, younger even than this girl in

my arms with wide gray eyes and soft cheeks, here to witness the burial of an ancestor who loved her but whom she will never remember. It might be young, but it is perfect. This is a place that is mostly sky, where a man used to flying could feel at home, a place where a man who breathed order could savor the symmetry of the rows and lushness of the lawns, a place full of promise, a place full of retired strength, a place with its arms wide open to heaven. It is hard to stand here and not look up to the sky, to the enormous blue atmospheric window above us. As I do, two planes carve hard contrail stripes across the blue, climbing fast with the sun sparking on their distant splinter-size wings.

It is our turn, those of us left behind by Lawrence Greensides, to roll our cars forward to the open shelter where the service will be held, across from the first pioneer stones in their tight rows. And so we do—cousins who have not seen each other in years, great aunts and great uncles meeting new nieces and nephews at a funeral, the assembled living remains of one man.

Our cars crawl.

 ᶜᵒ

Man is born to trouble (as the sparks fly upward). And Job would know. He knew trouble like most people know their beds. He tossed in it. He couldn't escape it. Death, disease, pestilence—trouble heaped up in heavy piles to break him. He was pushed down under those waves, all the way down until his wife was cursing and his pious friends were rebuking him, down until his children were gone, his wealth was gone, his health was gone, down like a submarine dropping into cold nothing, dropping toward his crush depth, toward the absolute breaking point of his righteousness, down until all he had was . . . The Whirlwind.

Only two men and one woman have ever lost more than Job.

Adam. Eve. Adam II.

Heat rises. Man is born to trouble. When Job lifted his face to the Storm, when he asked and was answered, he learned that he was very small. He learned that his life was a story. He spoke with the Author, and learned that the genre had not been an accident. God tells stories that make Sunday school teachers sweat and mothers write their children permission slips excusing them from encountering reality.

Lions are fed. Every day, animal stories end in those jaws. Leviathan snorts fire. Unicorns won't plow. What good is a story without struggle? What good is a plot without danger? How is a character's mettle tested? How is it made in the first place?

Nails are forged for pounding. Man is born to trouble. Man is born *for* trouble. Man is born to battle trouble. Man is born for the fight, to be forged and molded—under torch and hammer and chisel—into a sharper, finer, stronger image of God.

Eve had done nothing wrong. Our mother wandered the

garden, doing no evil. She and her lover existed in Paradise. What had she done to deserve a dragon? A serpent? A forked lying tongue and lying eyes laboring to *get her killed*?

She had been born. Her life was a story. She was born— even when pure—for trouble.

Ponder this. Adam. Our unfallen father arrives on the scene to discover what exactly?

Adam was given the world and a garden and all manner of fruit to eat. He was given every beast to tend and name. He was given a wife and lover traced by God's own fingers—a muse to make Helen of Troy put on sunglasses and a hoodie in shame. Fairy tale. And then, having done nothing wrong at all, he was given a dragon, a wife who had been deceived, who had believed that God was a petty liar and had therefore chosen to defy Him. Eve had stepped directly under the curse of the Almighty, smack into *thou shalt surely die*. Adam, still having done no wrong, had been given loss. He had been given trouble with a capital T. And like every person who has been given a beating heart and breathing lungs and seeing eyes and hearing ears and fingers and thumbs and thoughts and an entirely unasked-for existence in the flowing stream of history on this space-time stage, he had been given a choice.

As the sparks fly upward, Eve was born to a moment in the garden when she faced a dragon spewing lies.

As the sparks fly upward, Adam was born to a moment when his garden was invaded by a deceiving dragon and he learned that his love was under a death curse.

The plot hinged. The past was ready to be written in forever stone. The future waited to swirl up or down, left or right. Things would be now or things would be never.

He was born to it. Life is a story. Or didn't you know?

For some reason, there are people who seem to think that this means they have been born into *The Sound of Music* (the G-rated musical, as opposed to the actual events, which were a hard R), and they try to gloss over and completely avoid incredible darkness (both internal and external), by means of shiny faces and a chipper soundtrack.

There are other people (frequently raised in families or churches from the above category) who think that living life like a story means cultivating intense aesthetic snobberies (in an anti-Walmart, pro-Apple kinda way), never cleaning the bathroom in one's apartment or one's soul, fighting with one's roommates, and sucking down smoke over cheap scotch in plastic cups while thickly sprinkling f-bombs all over a late-night poop-pastry of pensive poseur philosophy with digitally downloaded despair providing the soundtrack. But only because they're realists, right? Only because they are the hard ones, the bright ones, the ones with too little sense of smell and too much sense of self.

(Guess which ones I have more experience with?)

As it turns out, there is a difference between asserting that life is a story and actually living life like a story. And there is another difference between living life like a story and living life like a good story.

Eve lost more than we can imagine. Adam was willing to lose anything, to sacrifice everything (even God), so long as he didn't lose her. Well, almost everything. He wasn't ready to give up himself. A delayed suicide pact is easier than an immediate sacrifice.

Story: a linked thread of occurrence, real or fictitious, in, around, and after trouble of some degree or sequence. Examples: WWII, *Goodnight Gorilla*, and all of reality.

Good Story: a linked thread of occurrence, real or fictitious, in, around, and after trouble of some degree or sequence, in which the triune nature is consistently revealed with artistry either through the real actions and choices of particular characters, the author's direct participation, or through the author's indirect judgments latent in the choices of style and arrangement in the recounting. Examples: WWII, *Goodnight Gorilla*, and all of reality.

Or something like that. Ish.

Your life will contribute to a grand and wonderful story no matter what you do. You have been spoken. You are here, existing, choosing, living, shaping the future and carving the past. Your physical matter and your soul exist, not out of necessity, not voluntarily, and not under their own strength. There is absolutely nothing that you or I can do to guarantee that we will continue to exist. You aren't doing anything that makes you be. We aren't the Author. You and I are spoken. We have been called into this art as characters, born into this thread of occurrence tumbling downstream in the long Niagara of loss set in motion by the trouble that faced our first father and first mother. We will contribute to the narrative. But how?

Would you like to be an orc? A ghoul? Plenty of people are. How about Gollum? He got a fair amount of screen time.

Would you like to be Adam, dooming your descendants with the thunder of your own folly?

Would you like to be Eve, the first to welcome darkness into your home, the first to embrace the biggest lie?

Here we are, with our feet on a path given to us at our births. Born to trouble.

The prophet Jeremiah wished that he had never been born. Solomon, the richest, wisest, most thoroughly married man in history, said that our lives are but vapor, that our days are full of sorrow, and that while greater knowledge is a greater burden, we should still get wisdom. We should grow, knowing that our burden will grow with us.

In Ecclesiastes, Solomon faces the Whirlwind. Where Job stood in loss, Solomon stands in plenty. Both stare at the tininess of troubled man, both face the massiveness of the transcendent Artist.

Trouble, trouble, boil and bubble. Read the Psalms. Bones melting. Dogs raging. Traitors traiting. The dust of death. Liquid joints. Vanishing strength. Doom. Hardship. Destruction. Humiliation.

From Psalm 60: "You have made the land to quake; you have torn it open; repair its breaches, for it totters. You have made your people see hard things; you have given us wine to drink that made us stagger" (vv. 2–3 ESV). (The KJV says that God has made us drink "the wine of astonishment.")

Doing a theological study on trouble is simple. Open your Bible to the lefternmost page and begin reading until the tail end when John the Revelator wraps up with a pledge that if anyone adds to his words, then God will add the plagues of Revelation to their lives, and if anyone removes any of his words, then they can just plain go to Hell. Amen (sings the choir).

Life is a story. All of it. From left to right. Including your bits. And at first, your greatest obstacles will be internal; they will come from pious misconceptions, religious platitudes and parallel assumptions, simplistic professorial rants vaguely remembered from freshman year, or just plain American ignorance.

Set them down. Read the Christian story.

Chalkboard please . . .

Assumption One: Paradise was easy living. Incorrect. It was joyful and glorious, which is a very different thing. Adam and Eve were given an entire planet to tend. Every last creature to identify, name, and oversee. Or, in the case of the dragon, identify, name, and kill. All before the fall. All while the world was perfect. Adam and Eve were not in hammocks, relaxing in the light of a perma-sunset with even tans while sipping on honeysuckle bouquets proffered by miniature ponies. They were given a job so big that only

Noah and the disciples who received the Great Commission saw anything like it. Adam's hands would have blistered and grown thick callouses. He would have sweat and bled and worked six days and rested one day every week through millennia. He would have done it with joy, with laughter, with a wife and children to labor and triumph with him. Yes, *triumph*. Because he was also given enemies. Big ones. Bigger than your roommate or that annoying rival in the adjacent cubicle. Fallen-angel-level enemies.

Assumption Two: God only cares about spiritual things. To be honest, I don't even know what this means, but those elusive *spiritual things* have been helping Christians cop out of true holiness for centuries. We are all like accountants with wizard-like abilities, funneling our choices and goals and actions through shell corporations and off-shore banks of unrighteousness. God only cares about spiritual things? His kingdom is a spiritual kingdom? Are you kidding me? God only cares how we emote at Him? That's part of it, sure, but I was pretty sure that He made physical animals and a physical man and gave him a physical job. I was pretty sure that He made a physical tree with physical fruit and told that physical man not to physically eat it or he would physically die. He physically ate it anyway and now we physically go into the physical ground, physically rot, and become physical plant and physical worm food. And because of this incredibly physical problem, He made things even more clear when His own Son took on physical flesh to lead a physical life that lead to a physical cross where He physically absorbed our curse, was physically tortured, and bought you and bought me and bought this whole physical world with His physical blood. If He'd wanted a spiritual kingdom, He could have saved Himself a huge amount of trouble (to say nothing of making the Greek philosophers and medieval gnostics a lot happier), by just skipping Christmas and the Crucifixion.

When men have an urge to physically do something they shouldn't, God suddenly has primary jurisdiction over "spiritual" things, which, when one really takes a thorough academic look at the question, means something foggy about our fellow man.

When the younger set would like to go along with a godless (but inevitably self-righteous) crowd, they encounter certain physical requirements. Welcome to dietary indignation, resentment of private property, the anathema of soda, and pious affirmations of a woman's right to kill (so long as she isn't killing polar bears with unholy diesel). Luckily—wipe brow here—God doesn't care about any of those things. Close one, right? I know. Phew.

Ink your skin and pierce your nipples. Get yourself a steady IV drip of guiltless self-affirmation. Serve dark urges and call them lovely. Demand that others feed the poor. After all, one can be a member of a spiritual kingdom and a totally different physical kingdom without any conflict of interest.

But whenever your physical urges fail you, when death

and pain arrive, discover the problem of evil and wield it widely. How could God allow you to feel physical hurt and physical pain?

Shrug. His is a spiritual kingdom, isn't it?

Back to the story.

Stories mean trouble. Stories mean hardship. The fall of man did not introduce evil; it placed us on the wrong side of it, under its rule, needing rescue. And God is not an aura ruling auras. His Son has flesh even now. You have flesh. This story is concrete, it is for real, and it is played for keeps.

In Genesis 3, after spiritual and physical rebellion, we have the levying of the great curses: God tells Eve that He will greatly multiply her sorrows in childbirth, and the itchiness of marriage shows up as well. (Man is born to marriage counseling as the sparks fly upward.) Adam is given toil and sorrow all the days of his life. The kicker here is not the toil, and not even the sorrow. *All the days of his life.* His life now has days—welcome to mortality and the ticking clock.

You will struggle and mourn and you will end. Dust you are and to dust you will return.

It is at this point in the narrative that Eve is given her name (because she will be the mother of all the living—or, by direct implication, all the dying). Eve is the mother of all those with limited days, all those who will toil and suffer and break down and die.

Your life is a story.

Your days are numbered. In the rain or the sun, in the

snow or as the yellow leaves fall, there is a day waiting for you that will be your last. You will return to the dust. Your birth scene will find its counterpoint. From this moment until then, you will live a story.

Eve did nothing wrong. She was born. She did everything right. And then the dragon . . .

Adam did nothing wrong. He had done everything right. And then a doomed wife and a dragon . . .

Job did little wrong. He was born. He did many things right. And then the dragon . . .

As for you (and I), well, I hope you like stories . . .

If life is a story (it is), and if we mean that in a deeper way than the average relayer of mantras (we do), and if we would like our stories to not merely play the role of miserable failures in the background of the broader story (off stage right), if we would like to live our stories well (check), then we must look first for narrative examples. Reading one's own story in real time and positively contributing to its creation (in real time) is much more difficult than reading something that has been written down and holding still for several ages. Start with the stationary stories.

Job did well. Job's wife? Job's friends? The devil tempting Job?

Adam, establishing the grand tradition of men everywhere, pooched it badly. But what should he have done? Step into the scene . . .

Careless self-absorption?

"Well," Adam says. "See ya, babe. I guess this is good-bye. I hope God makes me another one."

Or maybe he should get a wee bit self-righteous. We could pull that off.

"Eve! I can't believe that you could be so thoughtless. Don't you understand what kind of position this puts me in? Of course not. You were just thinking of yourself."

Or how about the vicarious villain?

"Seriously? You ate it?" Glances furtively at the spirit world, and then back again. Whispers: "What's it like?"

We, the strange human creatures raised on Bible stories, have frequently heard this story used as the classic model for abstention. Adam should have acted like a fourteen-year-old being offered pot for the first time. Right? Or maybe he should have abstained while also attempting to convince Eve of the error of her ways. He should have recommended that she apologize.

In the hopes of slightly improving our options, and like the good little literary critics we are, let's hop to another story about yet another man (born to trouble).

$e \sim$

Adam II did it right. Our Elder Brother, covenant head of a hijacked human race.

Jesus Christ was born to . . . what? Not trouble, surely. He was the Son of God. He was innocent. He'd done nothing to deserve trouble.

Jesus was born in a motel barn. To a teenage mother still slandered to this day. To an adoptive father who many believed (and believe) to have been a cuckolded nitwit. Jesus, the Word made physical, the Man born for trouble we cannot comprehend, was placed in a trough. He would trigger (but escape) a genocide. And he was just getting started. He would experience betrayal, profound brutality, and death before He even reached my own ripe age of thirty-four. He had come for exactly that reason. He had come for death, for a bride living (and dying) beneath a curse.

He was Adam done right.

Loosen your jaw and begin chewing, this gristle is tough. Adam, living in his story rightly, would have done the same. Adam would not have been the well-behaved Mormon teenager, abstaining from the fruit. He would have looked at Eve, seen her curse, seen her enemy, and gone after that serpent with pure and righteous wrath. He would have then turned to face the pure and righteous wrath of God Himself (that Adam had just imaged), and he would have said something quite simple, something that would be said by another, thousands of years later.

"Take me instead."

Adam could have been conqueror rather than conquered. Regardless, fallen or unfallen, he was born to die.

So are you. So am I.

Life is a story. Why do we die? Because we live. Why do

we live? Because our Maker opened His mouth and began to tell a story.

∽

My Marisol Helen is named for a great-grandmother who is, at this moment, only hours out of her own earthly chapter. My girl is two and eager to climb up onto me whenever I dare pop the lever on my recliner to better ponder the ceiling. She wriggles her way up onto my chest and then takes my unshaven face in her small, cherub-caricature hands.

"You tell me story," she commands. Her siblings call her the boss of the world. I raise my eyebrows at her and smile, waiting to see if she adds at least the politeness of a question mark. She does.

"You tell me story?"

I nod, and the hands leave my face. This is how she settles in. She widens her eyes, pinwheels excited fingers in a quick spasm of thrill, and then thumps her tiny elbows onto my chest and props her meringue cheeks on her hands. Her whole body is tense as she waits, her ribs shivering on mine.

"A bird story," she says. Other times it's a kitty-cat story (never a happy one) or a pirate story. Dog stories are common as are sibling stories and cousin stories and papa stories and Jesus stories and Marisol-with-wings stories. I let her select the genre and she does it well.

In every story, the stage is set, some little Eden of backyard trampolining is established before trouble (evil owls, sky pirates, a dragon, wizards, wolves, sharks) comes to ruin everything and threaten destruction. In every story, salvation comes. But just once (I swear), I wove it differently.

The world was happy. Marisol was playing with her animals in the backyard and they were all having so much fun. And then Billy the Bear and George the Monkey and Moo-Moo the Statue of Liberty Cow all thought it would be so much fun to go inside and have a tea party, and Marisol thought so too. So they all went inside and went upstairs and had the best tea party ever. Everyone loved it.

"The end!" I grin and spread my arms.

Her young eyes narrow above her propped-up cheeks. She exhales slowly, gives me a quick courtesy smile, and then grows serious.

"You tell another one," she says.

Dear Mr. Father,

Thank you so much for your submission of *From Trampoline to Tea Party*, but I'm afraid that it doesn't fit in our lists at this time.

Best of luck,

Marisol Wilson

Acting Editorial Director

I told her another one. She was almost eaten, and she loved it.

Ask her about the dragon sometime. She'll tell you what Jesus did to its head.

Dear Mr. Hipsterelli,

Thank you so much for your submission, but I'm afraid we already have several million pending volumes of peer-conscious faux-introspective pride on a bed of sexual guilt layered beneath a thick Crisco frosting of everything-is-going-to-be-fine-if-my-jeans-look-good-and-my-band-selection-is-appropriate. But do please resubmit if you should choose to live otherwise.

Best of luck,

Marisol Wilson

Acting Editorial Director

If life is a story, how shall we then live?

It isn't complicated (just hard).

Take up your life and follow Him. Face trouble. Pursue it. Climb it. Smile at its roar like a tree planted by cool water even when your branches groan, when your golden leaves are stripped and the frost bites deep, even when your grip on this earth is torn loose and you fall among mourning saplings.

Shall we die for ourselves or die for others?

For most of us, the question is rarely posed in our final mortal moment (although there is glory when it is). Death is the finish line of this preliminary race. Shall we cross the finish line for ourselves or for others? The choice isn't waiting for us down the track. The choice is now.

Death is now. The choice is here.

Lay your life down. Your heartbeats cannot be hoarded. Your reservoir of breaths is draining away. You have hands, blister them while you can. You have bones, make them strain—they can carry nothing in the grave. You have lungs, let them spill with laughter. With an average life expectancy of 78.2 years in the US (subtracting eight hours a day for sleep), I have around 250,000 conscious hours remaining to me in which I could be smiling or scowling, rejoicing in my life, in this race, in this story, or moaning and complaining about my troubles. I can be giving my fingers, my back, my mind, my words, my breaths, to my wife and my children and my neighbors, or I can grasp after the vapor and the vanity for myself, dragging my feet, afraid to die and therefore afraid to live. And, like Adam, I will still die in the end.

Living is the same thing as dying. Living well is the same thing as dying for others.

Marisol Helen Wilson tucks me into my chair, fully reclined. She brings me a tiny blanket and fingers my eyes closed. She sets a Statue of Liberty Cow on my chest. I write stories; I can see the prophetic echo of what is to come. A time will come when her hands will not be so small, when she will do this again, but with more tears and a box, when I will have finished my race, when my strength will have been poured out, when I will have spent every beat of this heart and my lungs can no longer net me life from the wind, when this body will have been broken. I watch her working, chattering busily to herself as she does, imitating the love of her mother. I listen to my other children laughing at the table instead of doing their homework. When that time comes, they and the Author of my life story will know the truth. I know what I want that truth to be; I have an Older Brother with a bruised heel who has shown it to me.

Mari places her hand on my head, as bossy as ever.

This is my body, I think, may it be broken for you. And for my beloved in the kitchen with her blond hair bound into a fountain on her head as she slides calzones onto a hot stone in the oven, and for those future men and women making each other laugh and throwing pencils in the dining room, and for their children, and their children, and for children I will never know. May I live hard. To the dregs. May my living be grace to those behind me.

"You sleep," Mari says. "I tell you story."

She makes a pious face and bobs as she conjures a narrative, pin-wheeling her hands.

"Once, there was a princess. She died. The end."

I laugh. Mari races away. She's right, after all. She only left out the middle.

❧

The body that Lawrence Greensides used up with ninety-five years of living is in a silver box wrapped in a flag. I carry a corner. Voices are low. A larger flag, curling up in the wind, rattles its chain against its pole. I am supposed to have words for this. I am supposed to stand among the living and speak, but I am surprised by the knot in my throat, surprised by how futile any words of mine may be in honoring the divine speech that mattered—ninety-five years of story that led Lawrence Greensides from his birth to his death, that led him through wars and wounds, through hardness to faith.

Without his choices, without his living, without his courage, I and many others simply would not be.

When I stand up front, I look at my wife, at my sons and daughters. I will speak, though not well. But I am only a sportscaster after a game. I want to fill my words with honor, but what matters now is my own living, my leg in this relay. My dying.

Man is born to trouble.

Man is born to story.

(And the sparks fly upward.)

SEVEN

Eyes Back: 2

MULTI-TRANSLATION FIELD TRIP INTO EXODUS:

And if *any* mischief follow, then thou shalt give/pay/take/match/render life for life, eye for eye, tooth for tooth, hand for hand, foot for foot.

Simple enough. Helpful in an ancient judicial setting. Useful for shifting personal applications in the New Testament aeon. But what if it isn't a case of mischief? What if loss isn't involved? What if no one took my life? What if they gave me one? What if they gave me eyes, teeth, hands, and feet?

We clearly have a precedent here, establishing value. I owe my Benefactor big. I owe Him my feet, hands, teeth, and eyes. I owe Him my life. But I'm not going theological here (though I could). I'm going someplace quite simple.

The above passage has been (half jokingly) described as: "Do unto others as they have already done unto you."

Okay. And if they have done you nothing but good?

One summer ago, at the encouragement of my uncle, I took my camera and my wife and headed to my mom's parents' house. I had wanted to for a while. I had needed to.

Margaret Greensides was and is sweetness. But her memory has moved on, and even when it was sharp, she had ceded the position of storyteller to her husband. On my mother's side of the family, Lawrence Greensides was the spinner of tales. As a kid, I would beg for them. And I would beg for home movies. My sisters and I would watch our granddad wrestle out the projector and the screen and then dig through his closet shelf for the box of mysterious tins holding his captured strips on spools.

We watched the normal family things (Christmases, lake scenes, birthdays, and first dates), but we also watched the unusual. Scenes from the roof of the Vatican. Scenes from the cockpit of a B-17 on a combat mission over Korea. Flak. Fear, and even the view out of the bomb bay doors as roads and bridges blew.

My grandfather gave me a love of stories and love for living them, a love of courage and jokes and bucking systems. He gave me an appreciation for the beauty of film, for capturing the fingerprints of light in a scene and displaying it a lifetime later. I saw a version of him and of the world that I never would have otherwise. I saw my mother toddling around with her bottle. My grandfather gave, and I owed. I can't pay him back, but I can at least pay him by proxy, by gunning with a camera myself, by pointing it at him.

The summer before he died, I settled in on a couch, propped the camera on the arm, and went fishing for stories while my grandmother smiled and slept and laughed and my wife watched. I caught my limit.

Lawrence Greensides was the kind of boy who would turn into the kind of man who could combat fly in two wars.

A train came down from Saskatchewan, carrying a young family. Albert Greensides needed work, and they were headed to Santa Maria, California, where he knew people. Instead, stretching his short legs at a stop in San Luis Obispo, he got a job. Lawrence Greensides and his mother were pulled off the train.

When Lawrence was growing and running wild in San Luis Obispo, the old coots in town were vets of the Civil War. Young Larry, with his slick black hair and wide smile, hammered out a garden hoe, hacksawed the head into a spear, and went shark hunting in a row boat in the deep tide pools. Young Larry was given permission to bounce around an empty lot in a Model T Ford, and when it overheated and the radiator needed fluid, he had a bright biological idea. He and his friend took care of it.

Larry was everywhere and into everything. He built a small wagon (on metal roller skate wheels), hitched it to his goat, Napoleon, and sold old magazines off of the back. He was a true son of the Depression, unchaperoned and innovative (with callouses on his conscience). As he grew, so did his boldness (and so did those callouses). He was the fuse and the dynamite, the high-speed instigator that pulled friends along behind. In some ways, his younger brothers are blessed that they couldn't keep up.

The family moved to Sonora, and at fourteen, Larry talked a friend (Rudy) into jumping a train with him. At the tracks, he managed to hide Rudy from the sight of his mother when she came searching for him. He figured (sagely) that Rudy would pull a chicken if he saw his mom, and that Rudy's mom wouldn't have come just to deliver cookies—she was an obstacle to his plans. He got Rudy onto a train, greeted the hobos, and away they went.

The two of them roughed it in Yosemite for four months. All the while, wild Larry kept up a surprisingly proper correspondence with his own mother (Gertrude). After his death last summer, his own son found a small box that he had always seen but never been able to open when he was young. The box had been Gertrude's, and it held the old handwritten letters from her teenage train-hopping Lawrence.

Later, an old WWI pilot whined and bobbed through the sky and into Sonora. High school Larry immediately wanted to fly. He also wanted female attention, so football was a possibility. But it was a possibility that could get one's nose kicked sideways. Flying it was.

From beside my camera, I probe and prod to find details

in my granddad's memory that have been left undisturbed. A few things rise to the surface, but his memories have well-worn paths. The stories come with gestures and sound effects that I remember from other tellings, laughs and sighs that conclude each tale. There were times when he told me some of these stories before, but this time has a different tone. He has never been comfortable with his waning strength, with the burdens of age. He sprinted up his stairs into his nineties. Some of those old stories used to bring a sparkle to his eyes, a yearning to be young again, to be strong, to once again take the controls of a plane and hammer-head in the sky. Hair-brained schemes would be formed, new plans would percolate (and he would look at me like I was Rudy, ready to be taken on an adventure). But frustration would eventually come as the scheme faded, as he faced the exertion and glanced at his sleeping wife who needed him. And then we were definitely not putting the boat in the water. We were not going to meet on the Oregon coast with him pulling his trailer. He was not going to see Jerusalem again. Or Sonora. Or San Luis Obispo. Or the uppermost slice of the sky. But we could always fix some lunch. Google Maps would have to do.

But that last time was different. The yearning was more clearly pointed in the opposite direction. He was humoring me with stories of a life he no longer missed. He was sharing regrets and fears that he had never shared. He tried hard to keep me from casting him as the hero.

Aw, phooey. You don't want to hear this.

Yes, Granddad. I do. And so will my grandchildren. I will seat them on the floor as you sat us, and I will show them my movies and yours. And your stories will be more than a century old. In thirty years, your time at Guadalcanal will be one hundred years ago, and those young faces will be amazed like I was. I am giving to them as you gave to me. I owe you.

And so he tells me his sadness about his brother Jack, and his terror over the ocean during Korea, and shares his respect for his father, and tells me where to dig in Sonora if I want to find gold.

And then he tells me about the bomb that changed everything, the bomb that sent him flying with a shredded leg. And from that moment on, Providence is the star of the story—Providence and the kindness of strangers. And that thread runs right through the tapestry. It leads from that moment on that gruesome island in the South Pacific all the way through to two characters talking—a grandson and a granddad. That thread ran to his grave just one summer later. It ran down into his grave and through to the upper slice of the sky, to the man he is now, where he is now, and to the man that I am and the man I want to be.

But aw, phooey. You don't want to hear that.

The (Blessed) Lash of Time

BORROWED, BENT, AND STOLEN (IN PART) FROM PSALM 90:

Before the mountains were birthed, before the orbs were molded and bowled, before the world was pitched from star to star, before everlasting and beyond everlasting, you are God. Your breath called man from dust, and to dust your voice returns him. In your sight, the rush of a thousand years is but as yesterday, as the path through one night. You sweep men away as a flood; we are a dream, like grass flourishing in the cool morning and dry and withered when the sun sets. Your anger brings us to an end, and your wrath is our fear. You set out our evils before you, the sins we have hidden face the light of your presences. All our days pass beneath your wrath and our years end like a sigh. They are counted to seventy, or eighty for the strong, but they are all toil and trouble, they are soon gone, and we fly away.

On a September day in the year of our Lord 2010, James Irwin Wilson uses a cane and a son to climb the stairs to the podium in the front of a small white church. He turns and looks at us, his descendants and friends. He is eighty-two, and this moment exists for his beloved wife, Elizabeth Catherine. After fifty-eight years, death did them part.

"I haven't cried since the sixth grade," my grandfather tells us. He pauses. "I wondered if I would cry now." He seems to wait, curious if the tears will come. They don't. He continues, nostalgic about his bride, the mother of his children, the one he loved like no other, and his voice does not waver or tighten. When my turn comes, I know I will at least have to battle my throat.

It is easy to see a man in the weakness of age, physical strength fading as the sun sets on a life, and to fail to see behind him, into his past, beyond the battered cover and into the man's core. But this moment reveals all the strength that I have always known was in my grandfather. And then some. He is not trying to be strong. He is strong. The *trying* came when he was fifteen, on a country road with his stricken father (and in all the work that came after), on a burning ship in Korea where he should have died (but his survival became a revival).

Grandpa Jim needs a cane, but his faith has seen no decay.

⁓

Time flies. I should be ashamed of the cliché. I am a writer after all. But here's the problem . . .

It's true. (Nod sagely.)

Time really hauls some patookis. (That better?)

As a rule of thumb, when older people tell you something, believe them. It will save you the shock of discovering later on that they were right (and also helps you dodge their smug gloating).

My childhood memories don't distinguish years very well. The summers have blended into one (when I was small), and one (when I was tall). Christmases are also unified. Birthdays? Those are a little better, but I really wasn't doing much mental calculating. I wasn't filing things away with a cautionary warning to my ten-year-old self: "Hang on to this, Nate. Twenty years from now you might think you were twelve when this happened."

I was busy living. I enjoyed myself. My parents made sure that the appropriate information made it into my head at the appropriate times, and I did my best to make sure that every other minute involved climbing trees, digging, LEGOs, or complicated games and collective imagining with my sisters. And drawing.

Don't get me wrong. I remember specifics. But not

enough of them. And those that I do all appear on a large mental collage wall with a lot of jagged scissor edges and sticky glue, not on a tidy timeline useful for classrooms.

Some people have razor-sharp chronology distinctions to their memories. And some of them are actually more dogmatic than accurate.

Here's just one oddity about being people: I don't remember anything about showing up on this planet (and neither do you). I am here. You are here. Others have to explain it to me. I take it on faith.

Everything that I believe about my own origin and the early years of being me, I have heard secondhand. I was clearly a free agent (based on the stories). I was assessing things and making decisions and taking action (with an emphasis on self-interest). I was living life to the fullest. And all of it is gone, at least from my memory.

But humans are not intended for data storage (though we have that capacity). We are intended for living, for moving through a story.

Question for a marathoner: Do you remember your fifty-seventh step?

Unlikely. But that doesn't cheapen the step. We know that it existed and it carried them forward. Shorten the race. Ask a miler. Ask a 400m specialist.

We fight to remember. We lose. But it's worth it.

Do I remember sitting on top of the fridge in early-morning darkness, digging through a box of green pears placed up there to ripen for canning, test biting each one? I think so. At least, in my mind, I can see the kitchen beneath me and my older sister looking up. But the story has been told my entire life. More likely than not, I am remembering a film adaptation of the incident, produced by my imagination.

But then every memory is produced by my imagination. Even moments in the present are conjured in the mind. Our senses collect, collect, collect, then translate into electrical signals firing like lightning through our nerves. Our minds receive, interpret, collate, and imagine just a fraction of a second behind real time. And, obviously, when our imaginations work with radically less (or decayed) information, things get . . . foggy.

Do I remember being two, awake, and hungry, and crossing the hall into the dark parental bedroom to awaken my mother (with suggestions of banana)? Yes, in the same blurry impressionistic way in which we remember dreams. Except for the banana part. That part I know I was simply told. But my body (if not my imagination) remembers those banana binges well enough to have formed a permanent aversion. I still loathe them.

I do remember this . . .

I am on my belly in a bedroom in a duplex. The carpet is the color of pea soup and has felted with traffic and age. My flimsy hollow core door is open. My right leg is kicking the floor beside my closet. My arms are crossed beneath my chin not too far from one leg of my bunk bed. I am studying a cowboy.

This cowboy is excellent. He is taller than most action figures, and he has a soft plastic vest, soft plastic chaps, and a soft plastic holster holding a hard plastic revolver. Hats and boots also included, but not as important. And his horse manages to stand with stability on the uneven carpet. Even now, I can feel the strap of the saddle in my fingers as I stretch it beneath the horse's belly, and fiddle it into place. The high point of the whole affair is attached to the saddle—a long, tassled, soft plastic rifle holster. I slide a compelling Winchester in. I pull the Winchester back out. Joy ripples through me.

The cowboy is placed in the saddle. There are reins to hold, but he chooses to hold his guns. And now I slide back and observe.

Everything here is a shade of brown—horse, man, boots, guns. But the sun has been dropping while I worked. The high window in my room is in the west. And now, at this moment, gold is pouring in and encasing my cowboy in a rigid slice of light. It is around the horse's hooves at first, gilding the split-pea carpet. It will move up, but I am impatient. I move the cowboy and his horse all the way into the light. Don't they always ride toward sunsets?

C. S. Lewis talks about *northerness*, about an overwhelming bittersweet yearning that bleeds into joy. For him, that sensation was triggered by cold, clear nights and

stars and wind in moonlit trees—it was connected to some-
thing stark and harsh and beautiful. Thus, northern. I know
what he means. The sensation of basking on a white beach
with a cold drink while observing Caribbean waters lapping
at the sand comes with its own beauty. But standing on a
cliff watching an angry gray sea pound the rocks? Tasting
cold salt on your lips from the spray while the wind lashes
your legs? Those moments in life when we realize that we
are standing in open jaws, when we feel so small that it
arrives with a dominating immenseness—when the stars
are suddenly no longer twinkly things, but massive seething
explosions punctuating an unimaginably cold and near-
infinite nothing—those are the moments when we feel our
true size, our true pitiful (feed me three times a day, keep
me breathing, beat my heart once a second, don't let me stay
underwater for too long, don't let me get hot, don't let me
get cold) dependence. Those moments are when we yearn.
That yearning, that groaning against the curse, that desire
to feel all that can be felt in a given moment, is how I think
of northerness.

The first time I felt it, I was on my belly, looking at a
plastic cowboy in the sun. I couldn't have been more than
four years old. It wasn't the cowboy that got me, though he
paved the way. That moment was the moment that I discov-
ered motes of dust in the air.

I was content. My happiness was deep. And then, slowly
at first, I learned that *deep* was still shallow. Happiness could

run straight down for miles. There was more of it down there than I could ever grab. The gold slice of light haloing my cowboy was full of tiny floating worlds, and every one of my breaths sent them swirling in a storm. I remember sliding my face beside my toy and trying to look up the beam of light to my high window. The motes were uncountable. They were lazy. They were happy, and when I held out my hand, I couldn't catch them. Even when I held still, they wouldn't land on my skin, but drifted away like tiny, confident fish.

I was small. The dust made me feel smaller. And it thrilled me. I returned to my toy, loving it and the dust and the light and the rug. Loving the texture of the soft plastic rifle holster and the perfect way the rifle slid in and slid out. Tininess. Yearning. Joy.

And from there, the scene continues unremembered, one step retained between many steps forgotten on the long (and too short) race to where and who I am. In all likelihood, plastic enemies arrived and there was much shooting.

I remember making a cardboard tomahawk in preschool (and then obliterating said tomahawk on a closet door in which my sister had taken shelter).

I remember the bizarre sensation of discovery when my older sister was given her own bedroom. I was led to a door in the hall that I had never opened and waves of amazement washed over me as it suddenly revealed a room that I had not known existed. I was three.

I don't remember one particular lecture from my entire

senior year of high school. And maybe a couple *en toto* from my time in college. But those lectures happened to me. I engaged with them in the moment. They were never meant to be permanent.

My wedding day is foggy. I remember being famished, stuck in a tux, making an emergency Burger King run, and waiting approximately forever for things to actually get rolling. As for the ceremony, the flower girl sprinted, the ring bearer took off his shoes, and my young cousin fell out of the front pew onto her head.

I don't remember the homily. I don't remember the vows. But they happened.

I remember my bride. I remember taking her hand. I remember the light slicing through the tall windows into the sanctuary and the feel of her dress as I slid my hand around her waist and the smell of her hair (rain), and the red of her shoes, and the permanence of her smile.

I remember an argument with a highway patrolman when I was supposed to be at the rehearsal more clearly than I remember the actual service.

The world never slows down so that we can better grasp the story, so that we can form study groups and drill each other on the recent past until we have total retention. We have exactly one second to carve a memory of that second, to sort and file and prioritize in some attempt at preservation. But then the next second has arrived, the next breeze to distract us, the next plane slicing through the sky, the next funny skip from the next funny toddler, the next squirrel fracas, and the next falling leaf. Our imaginations are busy enough capturing *now* that it is easy to lose *just then*.

But some moments cut so deep they cannot be forgotten. They scar (for good and ill). They usually touch life itself, or some glimpse of what life could and should be. Or the opposite. Starting lines and finish lines; glory and grief in between.

Time is . . .

A) an ever-rolling stream.

B) conjoined with Space in a wrinkly continuum.

C) unkind.

D) happening regardless.

It is the motion of Time that set Solomon's sage head peering after vapor. It is Time that makes life "vanity," that beats the drum of seasons, that creases your face and wipes your mind and stops your heart in the end.

Time is . . .

E) the velocity of life.

F) the pace of reality's narrative.

G) story.

Imagine a world that is truly and intrinsically and explosively accidental. Explain time in that world, in the world with no narrative and no narrator. Why time? Why progression? Before hydrogen had its alleged and infamous cosmic hiccup, did something aphysical and philosophically flammable snafu first? Perhaps nirvanic nothingness is more unstable than we thought; after all, it would have to spontaneously generate *progression* and *causation* (as laws and/or authoritative patterns) before hyper-hydrogen could get flatulent and before that flatulence could begin seeking radically sophisticated order. (Sidenote: By nirvanic nothingness I mean *nothingness*—*nothingness* as in what your teeth see only less, nothingness as in take a glass and empty it, erase the glass, remove the table on which it sat, part the electrons in the air where it once was and step between them into the black coldness of space, and then remove the cold and the blackness, remove the ability of anything to take up space, remove space, remove causation, and while you're at it, remove God.)

But we're not done. We need an emptier grasp of this concept. Nothingness (no space, no time, no spirit): Grab a book about talking mice. Stare at the cover. Ready? Turn to page number −77. Right. Now set a bowl of fruit at its feet or pull the beating heart out of a slave on top of a ziggurat in its honor because that bit of nothing (all nothing is one in its noneness) invomitvented causation, space, time, you, me, and herpes. And if it could do that, there's no telling what could come from its nonexistent bowels next. Nonexistence is the squirreliest of b$%^gods. Any nothing any nowhere could suddenly become *any* something *any* somewhere—and it could arrive with new laws for its new reality. Watch out for −77. It gave and it can taketh away.

Atheist Fortune Cookie: There is only the material world. Don't ask me where hyper-hydrogen came from, but I am pretty sure it blew up because I'm here (I think). The "laws" of nature and reality and logic and morality are non-binding and are merely internal descriptions of the accidental explosion by another part of that same explosion and are likely to further explode or implode into something else as stuff continues to splatter around. You have no soul, and love and loyalty are chemical by-products of the accident and have no authority as the explosion neglected to accidentally create any. You have no purpose, no deeper meaning, and are no more valuable than any other mobile composting machine, engulfing and expelling until you are engulft and expelt. Also, as you have no soul, the concept of *you* is itself shaky, as your self-identity is simply the result of an arbitrary atomic boundary imagined by static electricity in spongey tissue inside a spherical bone that appears to be proud of any carbon-based meat that happens to be electronically connected to it. You're not important. Your molecules prefer fragmenting to binding and will inevitably and absolutely fly apart. So suck on that, sucker of thatness. Also, you should be open to new opportunities this month.

Atheists trapped in an exclusively physical philosophy must maintain that what we have dubbed Time is just one part of a *physical* entity (thus, wormholes and bad TV).

Time is just another part of the shock wave perpetually spreading out from an explosion, ever impregnating nothing with something as the growing anti-crater we call a universe does its from-everlasting-to-everlasting belching.

My atheist friends: You aren't taking this seriously.

Me: What was your first clue?

Mystic Docs and Post-Docs of the Most-Low Goo: You are petty, simplistic, and ignorant.

Me: Page number –77 made me that way. Accept me.

*   ❧

Enough. Seriously people. For reals. What is Time?

How am I supposed to know? I can't even tell you what light is, and it's substantially more, well, substantial than Time. But that doesn't mean I won't try. There are some things I can say. Some things I think I can say. Some things I know (by faith), and some others I think I know (by indirect faith, faith in the tools given to us by the One in whom we have faith). I have a mind and I have senses and we have the patterns of deduction and induction. Most fundamentally, we have the personality of our Author revealed in all the places we can directly see (if our eyes are wide), and we can know with absolute certainty (by faith), that His personality will consistently extend into those places we cannot see. But now I'm just stalling on the high-dive like that fleshy kid in swim class. May as well jump. It won't sting any less after extended whimpering.

Time is that harsh current that thrusts us down the rapids of narrative causation. Every moment leads to another moment and those moments pile together, boiling and rolling in falls, creasing skin and blinding eyes and breaking bones and wiping minds. Why are we old? Because we were young. Why do we die? Because we lived. Why am I here? Because I was there. You cannot stop yourself from aging, which is to say that you cannot sub out of this extremely rough, full-contact (no pads) game. You cannot throw a diva fit backstage in this production and force the understudy to take your place. You are in every scene. You are on the field for every play. And you go into the next one and the next one and the next one carrying the baggage and the wounds and the weariness of the last one and the last one and the last one.

Time is rough on mortals. That roughness is what sent Solomon to his pen. Read Ecclesiastes and feel the ache he had in his chest as he, the most powerful potentate on his half of the planet, chased after the vapor of life with words, unable to capture time and slow it down, but able to grasp futility, because all we need for that is empty hands.

Everything old people say about time is true. For starters, it flies. As a kid living through semi-eternal summer vacations, this is hard to believe. But as an adult? Get married. Have children. And then sit back, stunned, watching an absolute roar of gorgeous moments and hilarious moments and exhausting moments disappear—quickly and in tragedy or marching off at the traditional pace, but disappear they must. Snap a photo or two. Read verses about futility. Watching one's small humans age and grow up packs a serious punch. It's like being stuck in a dream unable to speak, like being a ghost that can see but not touch, like standing on a huge grate while a storm rains oiled diamonds, like collecting feathers in a storm. Parents in love with their kids are all amnesiacs, trying to remember, trying to cherish moments, ghosts trying to hold the world. Being mortals, having a finite mind when surrounded by joy that is perpetually rolling back into the rear view is like always having something important on the tips of our tongues, something on the tips of our fingers, always slipping away, always ducking our embrace.

No matter how many pictures we take, no matter how many scrapbooks we make, no matter how many moments we invade with a rolling camera, we will die. We will vanish. We cannot grab and hold. We cannot smuggle things out with us through death.

Go to an estate sale (if you dare). Look for photos. Stare at boxes full of vapor untreasured. Leave quickly.

But this shouldn't inspire melancholy; it should only tinge the sweet with the bitter. Don't resent the moments simply because they cannot be frozen. Taste them. Savor them. Give thanks for that daily bread. Manna doesn't keep overnight. More will come in the morning.

Our futile struggle in time is courtesy of God's excessive

giving. Sunset after sunset make it hard to remember and hold just one. Smell after smell. Laugh after laugh. A mind still thinking, a heart still beating. Imagine sticking your fingers on your pulse and thanking God every time He gave you another blood-driving, brain-powering thump. We should. And we shouldn't, because if we did, we would never do anything else with our living; we wouldn't have the time to look at or savor any of the other of our impossibillions of gifts.

My wife and I tend to overgift to our kids at Christmas. We laugh and feel foolish when a kid is so distracted with one toy that we must force them into opening the next, or when something grand goes completely unnoticed in a corner. How consumerist, right? How crassly American.

How like God.

We are all that overwhelmed kid, not even noticing our heartbeats, not even noticing our breathing, not even noticing that our fingertips can feel and pick things up, that pie smells like pie and that our hangnails heal and that honeycrisp apples are real and that dogs wag their tails and that awe perpetually awaits us in the sky. The real yearning, the solomonic state of mind, is caused by too much gift, by too many things to love in too short a time. Because the more we are given, the more we feel the loss as we are all made poor and sent back to our dust.

Oh, but we notice heartbeats when they stop. And we beg for more. If we are capable of sulking about Christmas while still around the tree half-buried in shiny paper (and we are), then of course we are capable of weeping when Christmas appears to be over. The ungrateful always farm bitterness in their hearts. Those with faith (yet another gift) rejoice even at the end and after. They wipe tears, more profoundly feeling the full wealth of lives given when those same lives are lost.

⁓

I am putting my wife on a plane to honor her departed grandmother. Her heart ran out. I have just come from a viewing of the body that belonged to a close friend's father, peaceful and empty and used up. His heart ran out young. His very young grandchildren peered into his open box, looking at a gift that was ready to be packed away—a gift they will treasure even more when their still young memories fade.

Clichés are true. Time flies. You can't take it with you. You don't know what you got till it's gone. Dust to dust.

In the ground, we all have empty hands.

Enjoy life now. And now. And now. Before the nows are gone. See the gifts. Savor the food, knowing that you will have to swallow.

Two sidenotes:

Uno. Some people are given more on this earth and some are given less. Some people spend their days in pain with bodies that keep the yearning front and center, that keep loss always in the mind's eye. Widows. Orphans. The sick. The damaged (by birth or by man). Know this: God has special promises for you, and He loves bringing triumphant resolutions to those who have tasted the deepest sorrows. And this: Gratitude is liberation. We are all mortals, called into this narrative in this timestream without our consent. And we will all reach an end. See the gifts. And if they seem sparse, start counting. Omit nothing. Can you count that high? You may have less than others do, like the widow with two small coins in the temple. God had given her little, but what did she do with her little?

Dos. Grabbing will always fail. Hoarding always fails. Living to live always reaches inevitable and pointless Darwinian burnout—bigger fears, deeper mortal panic. Live to die. If you do, inevitable success awaits you. If you were suddenly given more than you could count, and you couldn't keep any of it for yourself, what would you do? That is, after all, our current situation. Grabbing will always fail. Giving will always succeed. Bestow. Our children, our friends, and our neighbors will all be better off if we work to accumulate for their sakes. If God has given you a widow's mite, let it go. Set it on the altar. If God has given you a greater banquet than you can possibly eat, let it go. Set it on the altar. Collect a ragtag crew and seat them. Don't leave food uneaten, strength unspent, wine undrunk.

Time strips us. Time keeps us from turning into mini-dragons, hunkering down on our piles of whatever we use to give ourselves some sense of worth. And when we go dragonish anyway, time knocks us off, and sends moths and rust and destroyers after our stuff.

Time motivates us. Sure, time counts up, but it is also a game clock, counting down. It is urgent. It makes *now* matter.

"Oh, we've got all the time in the world," says the man preparing to do nothing.

"This is due tomorrow!" says the woman suddenly finding intense focus.

Time is a kindness. We need it. We need loss to appreciate gift. We need the world chanting at us like a crowd counting down seconds at the end of a shot clock. Every day brings its own urgency. Every day has periods that expire, things that count down, and breaks to collect our thoughts, sip Gatorade, and draw up plays.

The sun is up! Get up, get up! Eat. Go, go, go! Eat again. Go, go, go! Eat again. Sit. Hold still. Maybe talk. Decompress. Then shut your eyes. Breathe weirdly while your mind wanders uncontrolled. And . . . the sun is up! Get up, get up! Eat. Go, go, go!

The grind. The wheel. The racing of the rats.

Time, the ever-expiring resource. Time, the thief. Time, the motivator.

Time, the finish.

Imagine being your flawed self without time. Stop shielding your inadequacies from observation, take a full beat, and dedicate a few of your precious seconds to giving the worst of your sinful impulses a two-eyed, unblinking stare. (I don't encourage people to do this often.) Think about your temper. Your resentfulness. Your lust. Your lies. Your selfishness. Your despair. Think about all the trouble you have on the inside. Think about the weight of that burden. I hope that it's a burden you fight, not a burden that has already conquered you. I hope it is a war, an advance, a struggle.

Now remove time.

There is no end to this race. There is no finish line. There is no final round to this brawl. There is no clock counting down.

You must struggle with that temper always. Forever. You will be seven hundred years old, still a lusting lecher weeping with guilt. A thousand-year-old woman who can't stop her poisonous tongue.

When young athletes train hard, a good coach is there. When they push themselves to dizziness, to vomiting, a coach is counting down.

You can do it. Just three more. Just five more minutes. Two more laps. You can do this.

And we find that we can. That we can push harder than we ever knew. Because once we have, we will be done.

Imagine running and running and running until your throat burns with welling acid from your gut and constricts with the sharp bursts of cold breaths that your screaming lungs grab and grab and grab to keep your body moving. Your coach is on the side. He shouts.

"It won't ever stop! You will never be done. Just keep going."

Me? I drop right there. Without a finish line, I quit.

In the ancient myths, Tartarus is where the rebel Titans were tortured forever, where they struggled to complete tasks with any end, without any completion.

Without death, without mortal time, this earth would be Tartarus.

Mortality is a consequence of sin. But it is also a gift. A mercy. A kindness. Death is grace.

A fallen and corrupt human race with no end? Dark burdens with no finish?

Because of death, we can run the good race. We can fight the good fight. Completion exists.

We made ourselves filthy and corrupt, and God "cursed" us with death like a mother cursing her mud-caked children with a scalding shower. His curse swallows up our own. Time marches us to Death, and together they strip our hands. But there is a Man there, beside the grave, collecting all our grime, stripping more than hands—stripping hearts (and minds and souls). He assembles a burden like no other. He ran His own race. And though He is the Son of God, He moved through time. For three decades He ran toward death. And when He reached it, He could say what all mortals needed said.

It is finished.

And He went, along with that burden, into a hole.

All of us die. Walk through the torn curtain and be scraped bone clean. Empty your hands and hearts. Die. Be made new.

Taste every one of time's moments. Swallow. Taste the next. Drink the water. Drink the wine. It is no good left in the glass. Sweat and struggle. Run. Fight. Receive. Give. Be grateful even for death, for the ticking clock counting down on you.

Seventy years. Eighty if you're strong. Less if you're like the Messiah. Look to Him and receive more grace. Stagger on. You can do it. Only a decade more. Or two. Or four. But there is a finish line. There will be an end to the weight on your back and the ache in your skull. This place is no Tartarus, and our God is no Scrooge. He gives without ceasing. Even when we fell, when our first parents defied Him, the first thing He gave them was an end, mortality, a path to resurrection, and the promise of a Guide.

And then He clothed them.

⟨⟩

On Saturday nights, our family gathers at my parents' house to eat and laugh and drink to grace. My sisters and their husbands come with their tribes and I with mine.

My grandmother, mother to my father, went into the ground on top of a hill two years ago. James Irwin Wilson comes to these Saturday dinners alone (and yet not). He is the one most likely to ask if he can invite an ex-convict, or to need a ride because he loaned his car (knowingly) to a thief, and now it is gone. His heart struggles. His blood struggles. The man who rowed at the Naval Academy now walks with a cane. The boy who was there when a stallion was rearing and his father was falling to the ground, the boy who ran a ten-acre farm and finished high school and worked eight-hour shifts every night in the Omaha stockyard is now eighty-five and not yet spent. Though he is trying to be. My grandfather has no intention of ending his life with closed fists. His hands will be open and they will be empty.

I began meeting with him early on those Saturday afternoons, and I set up a camera. He was uncomfortable that first time, because I was demanding that he talk about himself, and because he had forgotten to wear a tie. I laughed (in my sweater and jeans). He hasn't forgotten his tie since.

When he turned eighty-five, he asked for no presents. Like a good hobbit (though I have always said that he is more entish), he wanted to give to us. He is not in the business of accumulating, especially now, as he hears the crowd counting down. He had some birthday menu requests (with pie for dessert), and then he wanted to tell stories to his great-grandchildren.

That Saturday, aunts and uncles and cousins came, and when we had eaten and sung and laughed, we settled him in an armchair and sixteen great-grandchildren wrapped around his feet on the floor.

He had no doodads to give. No cheap party favors.

Instead, he gave those kids what they could never buy for themselves, what they could never find on their own. He gave them the memories of a boy on a Nebraska farm with brothers, a boy trying to break a wild prairie mustang. He gave them memories of his mother, born in a sod dugout in the prairie grass.

He gave a crowd of mostly small people (who all exist because of his choices in his moments) a glimpse at a time long gone, at moments extinct, at vapor seen with his eyes and remembered.

I—and all of those children—reap a tremendous daily harvest thanks to his faithfulness, thanks to the man with the cane who has received his life with joy, and whose large hands have always been open. thanks to the Author who crafted such a character and set him on his path, who claimed his heart and carried his burden.

For my part, as he sat and talked, I held a camera. A time will come, I pray, when I am the spent one in the chair still aiming to give. And if I reach his age in 2063, I hope, even then, to introduce this man to generations unborn, to give them more than words, but the flickering image of this face, and the sound of this voice.

On his birthday, this grandfather is not yet done. He has more wealth to give. He chose a passage of Scripture for each of his children and their spouses, for each of their children and their spouses, and for each of their children. Forty-six souls (and counting). He asked a son to arrange and print each passage on archive paper, and he wrote a note of marginalia to each of us, in the sharp, perfect handwriting of another time.

To the youngest of all, my sister's two-month-old son, he handwrote a simple message next to Colossians 1:9–12:

You may not remember me. I remember you and prayed for you when you were one day old. Great Grandpa

My sister cried.

My grandfather's accounts are in order. His seed is sown. His hoard is elsewhere, in the faces at his feet, and in the hundreds and thousands of stories his own story has touched and will continue to shape.

Drink your wine. Laugh from your gut. Burden your moments with thankfulness. Be as empty as you can be when that clock winds down. Spend your life. And if time is a river, may you leave a wake.

—— NINE ——

City Hiatus: Jerusalem

THE AIR IS COOL AND SLIGHTLY DAMP. I CLIMB, FOLLOW-ing the man in boots up a bank that would like to be a cliff, switching back and forth between and over brown stone and brown crumbly earth and green tufting growth, and discarded trash until we reach a flat lip of grass. We are already through the fence where people *may-not-go* and heading up onto the hillside full of things that people *may-not-open*.

But people do go here; proof lies among the empty bottles, too far from the fence to have been thrown. I look to my right, at the canyon across the road, packed and stacked with crumbling houses decorated with laundry and trash and wires, and divided by twisting, foot-packed roads too tight for anything but feet and bicycles and some of the sputtering motorcycles that I can hear from where I stand.

"Gehenna," the man with the boots says. His English is accented. His boots are nice. His hair is tossed. He is the expert. I have been dragged here to speak to him in front of cameras about first-century tombs and burial shrouds. He continues: "I don't know how familiar you are with mythology . . ."

I nod. "I know Gehenna. This place used to describe hell. All burning trash and outcasts."

It is his turn to nod. He walks forward, climbing up onto another grass shelf, leading me to a cliff's edge.

"Do you know of Molech?" he asks. I do, but he doesn't wait for my answer. "This is where many of the babies were being sacrificed. With the drums and the rituals, the priests would fly the babies from this cliff to be broken below. Many many thousands. So long ago." He smiles at me, shivering a little like someone enjoying a touch of spook in a movie. "Amazing, yes?"

Amazing? I find it sickening. Literally. Disgust sits in my gut like dough. I step closer to the edge and look down at the boulders, and at the modern asphalt that now stripes the base of this site of slaughter. Disgust can breed anger, even across millennia. I have babies—a daughter merely days old as I stand there on the cliff, on the opposite side of the world from where she and her mother wait for me. I saw my son dropped when he was new and his mother fell, and then she released him from only a couple feet and into mud before she tumbled and rolled. I saw his arms and legs tuck in tight as he dropped, and when I picked him up, and I held him, his rage was great and his hurt nonexistent. His arms and legs did not relax until he finally slept.

I am used to standing in places rich with history. I have hunted them. And usually, as the reality of those layered narratives coiled up to the present sinks in, I picture untold scenes playing out and time passing until, finally, I can only see myself, standing there groping blindly at an unseen past, conjuring history with my imagination. This is different. I am not imagining anything. Thousands of babies as real as my own died in this place, murdered by men as evil as any men have ever been.

The history is as heavy on me as a dentist's lead X-ray apron. It is in front of me, beneath me, and behind me. The place feels cursed.

I turn around and face my expert, booted, smiling friend. Behind him, up the hill, I can see the Eastern Orthodox monastery that has granted us permission to be where people *may-not-go*. I can see the puckered mounds of sod-swallowed tombs, the open mouths of those desecrated through the centuries. The small stone faces of tomb entrances that have not quite been overgrown by turf even after thousands of years.

"This place was called the Field of Blood," says the wearer of the boots, turning to lead me away.

"Wait," I say. "What?" I had known we were visiting a Jewish burial site, but . . .

"Judas hanged himself here. It was made unclean, good only for graves. Caiaphas buried his father-in-law here."

"Seriously?" I turn in place. Where was the tree? Where did he do it? "They literally bought this field with the thirty pieces of silver? It's been a graveyard ever since?"

My expert nods.

The lead apron on my chest doubles. I can't believe that he's serious, that he can actually know any such thing, but then where I live, history vanishes into oral legend anytime pre–Lewis and Clark.

The boot man is marching away uphill leading me toward the first-century grave he entered only weeks ago. He receives death threats for doing so, even though he opens no sealed graves—he only examines those defaced by the residents surrounding the valley.

I hop along after him, eyeing bigger empty medieval tombs as we go. He tells me that crusaders hijacked a few of the posh-est digs for themselves, chucking the Jewish bones out.

The sound guy and the camera guy are lagging behind. The director, I think, is yearning for a smoke.

I am supposed to be focusing on shrouds and burial practices. But I'm not. There are too many other far more interesting things going on in this city of peace that has been built of bones.

I wanted to get in a tomb.

Before I leave Jerusalem, I will climb into two (and a half). One (and a half) of them were real. The other . . .

The Church of the Holy Sepulcher was not what I expected.

I, noble Protestant quester for shrouds, step through the big heavy doors and into an atmosphere thick enough with incense that I can feel my eyebrows combing the air. The stone of unction is directly in front of me and set low to the floor so that people naturally find their knees. The slab of stone—where Christ's body is said to have been anointed before burial—is shiny and damp. Smoking canisters are packed in tight above it, dangling on chains. A middle-aged woman is on her knees, rocking in place, mumbling Russian and taking one tiny icon after another out of her purse and rubbing each of them on the stone.

"So . . . ," the director says. She's blond and competent and British and an unbeliever. "We were thinking it would be great to get a shot of you maybe coming in, taking in the room, then crossing to the stone and kneeling before you touch it."

"No." In case my word is unclear, I also shake my head. "No way I'm kneeling."

"Why not?"

"Because the ghost of John Knox would haunt me. I'll touch it, because I'm curious, but I'm not kneeling."

This position of mine is not one that is easily understood. Why won't I kneel? I like the Russian woman on her knees. In fact, I feel like giving her a hug. But this is not the stone where Christ's body was anointed. If it was, I doubt I could keep my feet even if I tried.

The hard historical truth: this place has been razed down to small sling-shotable rubble multiple times through millennia. Most recently, everything in this place was reconstructed and replaced after a fire in the 1880s, including the stone of unction. And even that Victorian slab of wet stone has been replaced since then because millions of pilgrim hands and scraping icons literally erases the stone completely.

Cameras roll. I crouch awkwardly. I place my palm on the stone and rub its cold, oily surface, taking in the pilgrims all around me as I do.

The Russian woman has tears as she clatter slaps tiny frames out in a row and prays. This is an old game, the exploitation of the poor and simple by the beards and hats. It is a game that has made many a prophet groan, and I feel the familiar pit of anger growing.

Yes, I'm a Protestant. Yes, I have Roman Catholic and Greek Orthodox friends. Yes, we can argue about which limbs of Christendom have life and which are dead and brittle or dead and soggy and sprouting fungus, but long ago there was only one root—here in this city where wide-eyed disciples gathered around the Man with the hole in His side. If this place is real, it is the birthplace of the new humanity, the place where Behemoth had his nose pierced, where Leviathan was leashed, where the Seed of Woman shook the stars with His Triumph.

Which is why we Christians want it to be real so badly

that we're willing to fake it. Which is why enemies of the cross have worked so hard to keep it smashed—as if grinding down a hilltop and a tomb could undo the narrative, could unravel Victory itself.

Every rock is spoken by the Word. Every time I touch a stone, I am touching the Voice of God. Every cell of me is crafted by that artistry. My life is His breath. But we mortals grow numb. We want to feel more. And so we add MSG to our earthly brands of holiness.

The evangelical worship leader bounces on stage with his eyes shut, thumping his T-shirted breast—pushing, pushing, pushing people to feel as the chords progress. In Jerusalem, a freshly quarried rock is offered to pilgrims beneath trickling mystical smoke.

Lord, we flail. Forgive the lies we tell from purple thrones on TBN. Forgive the lies we tell in shrines. Forgive our every attempt at self-redemption, the holy efforts we call our own, all the clawing we call resurrection. Bury us. Take us to helpless dust. Then roll away that stone and call us by our names. Make us all Lazarus.

The experience around the Holy Sepulcher is tragically, comically surreal—stairs up to touch the tip of Golgotha there, stone of anointing here, the towering, teetering pinkish alleged tomb of the Messiah, site of *the* Easter, pivot of history, place where the stone rolled and the angel sat and Death was conquered, just over there. At least, it might be if it hadn't been built after the Mormons were in Utah, after Lewis (and his friend Clark) had taken their little walk through the hills where I live, after the American Civil War had already been fought and after New Yorkers were riding in elevators.

So, no, not the tomb of the Messiah.

But the Russian woman—she has more to teach me than this stone. I watch her hands, knowing that the Father knows every crease. I watch her face, knowing that the Father knows every grief. Every beat of her weary heart is spoken, every bit of her narrative is spun with the words of the Word. God is more than omnipresent; He is omnicrafting, and even though I have never felt further from Him than in this place, how I *feel* is irrelevant. He is here, and His image is in me, and in her—the woman panning for holiness with plastic frames around iconic cards scraped across a damp stone.

I want to say something to her. To smile and tell her that she need not fight so hard to be heard, that she can rest, she can be still, that she can be at peace. She can be known and kept and guarded without the struggle, because the Word stooped, the Word struggled and died and erupted in joy, and stones like this one were shattered.

She doesn't look up. She keeps rocking, like a child lost in a crowd, fear in every motion, abandoned by her father, unwilling to look anywhere but down.

"Good," says the director. "We got the shot."

I am angry.

❧

I *am* on my knees in the Field of Blood. The ground is soft from rain; the hillside is steep here and fleeced with green, every blade of grass beaded with water. I feed my hands through the small, uncovered hole where a stone was broken. Dropping onto my belly, I worm forward into the first-century tomb until my head and shoulders and arms are through.

To my left, a shelf, where until only weeks ago, bones had lain wrapped in cloth for almost two thousand years. Cut into the stone in the back of the tomb, a tiny door. On the wall beside me, a spider the size of a mouse. On the floor, deep standing water.

The man in boots taps my back and I wriggle a retreat. He will take me to another, one with less water.

I feed the next tomb my feet first. Twisting, pretending to be adroit, I grope for the floor with my toes and then drop all the way inside. Water splashes around my shoes, but rubble keeps them from completely submerging. The man in boots is ducking in the opposite corner.

This is my first time inside a grave. It will not be my last.

It is a small room, this chamber of death, an empty cube cut into stone. There are spiders here as well, and the body shelf. We talk about the first century, the man in boots and I. We talk about the small door and hallway cut into the back of the tomb. In a family tomb like this one, a body would be stretched out on the shelf until it had been completely decayed. Then the living would return, the tomb would be reopened, the bones would be collected and stored in the little rear hallway, leaving the shelf empty for the next in line to die. As families (or wealth) grew, additional chambers would be cut, additional shelves, additional hallways for bone storage.

There is a strange realness to mortality here, a realness hard for our modern ignore-mortality sensibilities to understand. I respect this way, but I prefer our own more permanent good-bye. Maybe because it is easier, because it enables us to scoot away from death quickly and focus on the photo albums. Revisiting the tomb to collect the bones and shelve them? Seeing the bones of those who have been shelved every time another member of the family dies? Knowing that you yourself would pass through decay on the same stone shelf where your ancestors rotted away, that your skull would eventually sit on a shelf beside theirs?

Oddly, there is a poetry there. For those of us who live in the young West, it is hard (or impossible) to remember our ancestors' names just four generations back, let alone where they are buried. We are nomads, still traveling and populating the open spaces, playing Johnny Appleseed with our people, rolling back the sod and saying good-bye. Or, more commonly now, burning them up and scattering the dust.

It could be healthy to stare at a row of skulls that march

back through the past, to remember that you are, in fact, a sequel and not a standalone.

Back outside, standing in the grass that God loves to grow, I look around at the swirl of story, at the blue of the sky and the racing clouds. I look at the puckers in the hillside where in the youngest years of AD men and women would slide into the rooms of the dead to tend the bones of the forgotten, arranging them in small libraries of lives.

Here, in the field where Judas hanged himself, the small details make me feel the momentousness of the story in which we all live and die. A bird beside a stone. A blowing piece of trash. A tree swaying as the journeying wind finger combs its branches. Away from the cage of pink marble and incense, away from the robed jailers of holiness, I can know (and feel) that I am standing in a city where the great story turned even more profoundly than that garden where the story first turned, in a city still troubled by the weight of its own story.

Thirty pieces of silver purchased this field. The same thirty pieces of silver purchased a Lamb to make Death pass over. And in doing that, those thirty coins helped purchase every field that has ever been made unclean with death, every place where ash has been scattered, every low mound of western sod where a seed has been planted and forgotten, every shelf where bodies went to bones, every cliff where babies were thrown, every clinic dumpster where they are still thrown, every peat bog and ice cave where men and women have ever been drained of breaths and beats and felt soul abandon flesh.

Thirty coins bought the Lamb that bought the world. The world, this Field of Blood.

—— TEN ——

The Quick, the Grateful, and the Dead

SOLOMON: ALL THAT GOD DOES ENDURES FOREVER. Nothing can be added to it, nor anything taken from it.

I am driving at night. My wife is asleep. My children are asleep. They appear inexcusably peaceful in the dashboard glow of our Yukon. I am perched on razors of awareness, with pressure tanks of adrenaline poised and ready to fire. We are climbing Mt. Shasta through an all-out high-altitude onslaught of snow. The pass was closing when we reached the base, but my vehicle conned the road block. They waved me through without looking at my tires—four rubber skis.

The interstate is under inches of sloppy wet snow and there are no tracks to lead the way. We are here, and so are

131

universes of snow. We are sliding. Constantly. But I want out of California, and it hadn't seemed so spooky at the base when all of this was just rain, when I had been as confident in my vehicle as that man at the roadblock.

I am blind. The blizzard is clogging my wipers and flinging back the brightness of my headlights with a million darting mirrors.

Thirty-five miles an hour is intense. But I grew up in Idaho—I know how to drive in snow. Although, apparently not. Any sage Idahoan would approach tonight with the same technique: stay off the roads.

Not surprisingly, mortality is on my mind. I am as focused as I ever was on a football field with the ball in my hands. React, react, react. Reverse. Slow. Turn into it. Accelerate. But those plays took seconds. We're already more than an hour and twenty into this one play, and I've been praying since the fifteen-minute mark.

If there are pull-offs where we could stop and sleep off the storm, I can't see them. And I'm not stopping on whatever I might think is the shoulder. It could be the centerline for all I know, and even if I found the shoulder I would still just be asking to be killed from behind.

I find a truck asking for exactly that. Two tiny pink dots appear in the flakes just off of my hood, and I have exactly no time at all to realize that they are taillights and that they aren't moving.

Fishtailing quickly, we slide out and around the truck. I

fight to keep us from swinging all the way around and out of control and we pass the truck sideways. I see the shadow of a man in the cab, watching us, before we manage to straighten out and ski on. He wasn't stuck. Not physically at least. I hope he moved. I hope he survived the night.

My wife sighs, stretches, and yawns.

"Hey," she says. "Where are we?" She looks out the windshield. "Can you even see?"

Yes. I can see the snow. I pat her leg.

"Go ahead and sleep, babe."

She does, and I'm extremely glad. Adding fear to this scene won't help.

༄

When fifteen-year-old James Wilson decided to break his wild Nebraska mustang, he waited until there was three feet of snow on the ground. His father had prohibited him from any such attempt. After all, James was the only one bringing in any pay and the only one tending the farm. He couldn't keep doing that with a broken arm or leg (or head). But the man was bedridden. There was nothing he could do to stop his son.

James saddled the wild horse and led him from the barn.

At lunch and after school, James had always been the target for fights. He was stubborn enough and big enough and friendless enough that someone always got "chose" to go after him. Once, when he was fourteen, two college boys pulled a car across the sidewalk and hopped out to confront him. James was with his smaller, friendlier, older brother at the time. The boys demanded that the two high school kids down some beer on the spot. Leonard politely declined, but James ran his mouth.

One boy held back Leonard. The other didn't stop until James was bleeding in the street.

James Wilson knew how to hold on. He braced himself and hopped onto his mustang. The horse bucked. And bucked. Twisting and kicking and rearing in the snow. James held on. He held on, exhausting the horse with his weight and his strength and the snow. The wild horse worked himself into a frothy sweat and still the boy clung to his back. Finally, the horse was still and the boy was still and both were panting and both were steaming in the cold. After a few moments of rest, James nudged the horse forward toward the drive. On the drive, he nudged the horse into a trot. From the trot, he kicked the horse into a run and rose in his stirrups. The broken horse galloped. The boy laughed. And then the horse stopped, locking his legs. The boy flew.

❧

Accelerating down a drop, I tap my brakes and feel the car slide. I tap them again, just managing to control our angle. Tapping and turning, we cross hidden lane lines, sliding fifty yards, seventy-five. No need to gallop. My heart slows as we slow. We're not flying off the mountain yet.

I am driving completely by faith now. But then, when am I not?

Not one of these flakes exists apart from God. This storm of molecules, of atoms, of matter made from nothing by the One whose words are made flesh, is no more or less crowded with His art than a fall day with a gentle breeze stirring slowly falling leaves down through layers of sunlight. His ability, His graciousness, His artistry, is just as present in both. But the two are showing different sides of His nature, of His joy. He is here, speaking, shaping, knowing. He is here, pumping my blood and sparking my brain and holding the tendons in my fingers in existence. He is as much on this mountain and in this storm as He is anywhere and in anything.

My children, my wife, and my Maker are all asleep in this boat.

I know the story. I don't want to make the same mistake as those disciples. How could they fear a storm if Christ Himself was with them in the boat? It wasn't difficult. At least it isn't for me. I am making their mistake. I know He is here. But with my heart stomping twin kick drums inside my rib cage, that knowledge isn't as easy to lean on.

~

I have switched tapes and adjusted the camera. I am the grandson raking the leaves of a granddad's life. But there are so many, too many. I cannot press all of these in a book or capture every moment because I cannot go back in time and mount a camera on my granddad for all ninety-five years of his life. While my grandmother sleeps, I ask Lawrence Greensides a simple question. When were you the most afraid? Anytime. Not just in the wars. But I am expecting the story of Guadalcanal. That story is one of the reasons why I am here, one of the leaves I want to capture and keep for generations.

My granddad requires exactly one long breath to find his answer. And a change washes over his expression as the memory arrives. This memory is carved in deeper than most. His whole body has tensed. He exhales slowly, pushing that tension away.

He hunted sand sharks with a garden hoe. In high school, he and his friends worked to time cars so exactly that they could both come at an intersection at speed and cross as near to impact as possible. They worked at it until the bumpers would click, throwing a spark as they passed.

Crazy. Clearly a future combat pilot.

It is stories like that one that make me curious about what would trigger his fear.

Not Guadalcanal. Not that near escape. And not even the next one, when the marines were evacuating an island and one man tossed him a .45 where he lay on a bed with a shattered leg, and he was left alone to listen to the approaching gunfire.

Korea. A long-range bombing run. The anti-aircraft had

been intense. The mission grueling and deadly. But his fear arrived with helplessness, not on the mission, but on the return. He flew into a storm.

After combat in the South Pacific, after watching marines bulldoze bodies into mass graves, after seeing friends fall out of the sky, after watching flak punch through his wings and his own engines burn, after landing with an undetonated explosive round sticking up out of his own wing, his greatest fear came at the hands of *weather.*

He stops looking at me as he tells the story; he is looking in front of him, at his invisible instruments, holding his hands flat to picture his wings.

That storm broke him the way nothing else had. He describes flying into walls of air like they were made of brick, having his nose thrown straight up before the whole plane was thrown sideways. He rocks back in his chair. Being crushed from above by air like a giant fist. He rocks forward. Hail like bullets. Lightning strike after lightning strike hitting his plane. His instruments shot, his radio useless, navigation impossible. They were beaten and battered until he was sure his wings would snap or his engines tear free. They dropped and were launched. His wheel jerked in his hands while lightning struck and he was sure the hail was going to come through the glass. He fought his plane down, trying to find the floor, trying to get beneath the storm. But the floor was the ocean and they had been shrapnel in the storm long enough that his fuel was drained. He stayed low, ready to ditch in the water when his tanks were empty. He found a single rock, jutting up from the sea, and began to circle it so his crew would at least have the chance of getting out of the water after the crash.

And then his radio chirped. His base had gotten through. He was given coordinates and he left the rock behind, climbing back into the storm.

He reached his base, but lost engines on descent. He landed a B-17 glider with empty tanks.

⁂

Me, I'm driving in the snow. I'm climbing what I hope is a final peak before I descend into Oregon.

As I drive, I shift my conversations with my Maker. I am no longer asking for safety, for alertness, for vision, and ninja reaction time. I shift into thanks. Thanks for the people in the back with the dreams, their lives depending on me. I thank God for all the times that I have been kept safe without even knowing. For the times my wife was kept safe and my parents and their parents. For this snow. For light. For storms. For fear and for the focus it brings.

When the snow flies in the headlights like stars at warp speed, when we stand next to danger we cannot control and feel its hot breath on our necks, when steam comes off of its sides and we can do nothing but hang on to the wild mustang, we are no more or less in God's hands than we have ever been.

How many cars have you ever passed on the road? How many headlights have snapped by you going the opposite direction? Millions. How many potential fatalities exist on every drive that you have ever taken? Hundreds (even on the short ones). We paint a line (sometimes) and agree to stay on opposite sides as we hurtle along in tons of metal flung by explosions. We fly through the sky strapped to turbines screaming with power and expect to coast down safely on the air.

We live on a ball of molten rock hurtling through outer space, invisibly leashed to a massive orb of flame. It is steered by Whom?

How many super-volcanoes have wiped us all out? None. How many earthquakes have killed us all? I'm still here. You? How many could have?

As the earth screams through space, balanced exactly on the edge of everyone burning alive and everyone freezing solid, as we shriek through deadly obstacle courses of meteor showers and find them picturesque, as the nearest fiery star vomits eruptions hundreds of times bigger that our wee planet (giving chipper local weathermen northern lights to chatter about), as a giant reflective rock glides around us slopping the seas (and never falls down), and as we ride in our machines, darting past fools and drunks and texting teenagers, how many times do we thank God? We are always in His hands, but we often feel like we are in our own. We can't thank Him for every breath and every heartbeat, but we can thank Him every day for not splatting us with the moon or letting us drop into the sun.

When a drunk crushes some family, some mother, some friend; when a story ends, then we wake up. Then we turn to God with confused expressions, wanting to know why He was sleeping in the boat.

He brought us here from nothing; is He ever allowed to take us to an exit? His own Son died young; do you think He doesn't understand? Moses didn't see the Promised Land. Samson died blind in the rubble. Stephen beneath stones. Paul without a head. Peter upside down. In a bed or on the battlefield or on asphalt in shattered glass beneath a flashing light, we are God's stories to end. How many drunks has He spared you from? Thank Him before you ask to be spared from another. How many breaths have you drawn? How many winter winds have tightened your skin? How many Christmases have you seen? How many times has the sky swirled glory above your head like a benediction?

See it. Hear Him. Thank Him. Ask for more.

Search for moments in your story for which you can be grateful.

In mine, two strangers changed everything. More than two. Many, many more. But two of them represent the others well.

Miss Smith, first name unknown.

James Wilson had scarlet fever when he was little. The family was quarantined, but when he was well again, he wasn't all the way well. He didn't speak until late and remembers weeping when his older brother shoved him into a kindergarten classroom and shut the door behind him. He failed frequently, and before long, he was four years behind an older brother who was only two years older. James was ten and fast becoming the ox, with the size to match his academic failure.

Miss Smith was eighteen. I wish I had a picture. She was a girl without college sent into a one-room schoolhouse out in the cornfields of Nebraska, five miles from the nearest town. And when she looked at James, she saw anger and embarrassment and an easy path before that boy's feet. As the soul of that little farm school, she met with James, heard his frustration, and read him well. How could he ever catch up? He was angry, embarrassed, hopeless.

She told him that there was nothing standing between him and the grades ahead. She promised him that she would teach him as fast as he could learn, and she was as good as her word. She worked with him until he was more than on pace. And when the family moved into South Omaha, it is thanks to Miss Smith that James wasn't hobbled, thanks to Miss Smith that he would be able to juggle his way through high school while running that farm and working nights in the stockyard.

I owe Miss Smith my life. (To whom do you owe yours?)

Thanks to her, James was academically aggressive, studying and testing into his navy enlistment to land a higher rank, testing into a Naval Academy Prep School from the fleet, and numbering among the fraction of students appointed to the Academy from that school.

As an officer, he sailed for Japan . . . and my grandmother.

A defeated ten-year-old boy stood at a narrative crossroads in a cornfield schoolhouse. An eighteen-year-old girl found him there. She picked him up. She pushed him. I exist. I don't even know her first name.

❧

I've had enough about the weather. I've switched tapes in my camera. I want the story of Guadalcanal.

Lawrence Greensides sat on the hood of the overloaded Jeep, racing to get off the airstrip before the bombs reached the ground. They lost that race. I don't know how many of those men survived, but I know that my granddad flew as the Jeep drove straight into an impact.

He woke up hundreds of yards away on the wrong part of the island, behind a log. Below the knee, his leg had been torn and snapped by shrapnel.

Someone had carried him.

I thank God for whoever that was. May God bless him even now.

Bombs were still bursting. Palm trees were springing into the sky in storms of fire and earth. Lawrence crawled toward a visible foxhole and down inside. He was well away from all the air force boys. He was with marines.

In the hole, he managed to turn and lean his back against the dirt wall. Another bomb rocked the ground right outside. A piece of metal shrapnel whistled into the hole like a ninja star and hit him square in the chest. It hit him exactly on the zipper of his flight suit and tumbled onto his belly, glowing and smoking. He brushed it off quickly, and panic set in. He was in the wrong place and he knew it. He had to move now. A marine stuck his head in the hole, and my granddad demanded that he get him out. More marines. They didn't want to move him. But they did. They got him out and into the back of another Jeep and they raced for the airstrip.

The last plane in Lawrence's squadron was turning to take off. Those marines in that Jeep dodged craters and ran it down. They tossed a wounded air force officer into the back.

I don't know their names. I don't know if they ever left that island. Their stories marched on through that valley of the shadow of death.

There are vets who enjoy a little rivalry between the different branches of service. But all my life, I heard my air force ancestor talk about marines like they were solid gold. Because they were.

On another island, my granddad's leg was set with the worst of combat medicine. A plaster cast was wrapped directly onto his skin (seventy years later he still had no hair on that leg), gangrene set in, and he was ignored. His leg was literally rotting in the cast hooked to the ceiling with fluid running out of it. He would shove a stick down the cast to punish the horrible itch, and flesh would come back out with it. Men were dying by the thousand. All the islands were threatened. He was one man with shrapnel wounds, rocked with infection. Nothing worth saving.

Until a medic from Brooklyn found him. In that chaos of wounds and mayhem of death, one man took that leg personally. He was the one who tore the plaster off (along with the hair and much of the leg), he was the one who went to war with the stench and the rot, he was the one who held back the hacksaws. Not content to save my granddad's life, he also saved his leg. He was the one who came into that room of despair with a laugh, a pack of cards, and confidence. Over and over again.

After the war, Lawrence Greensides searched for him. Grateful, he tracked him every way he knew how. More than seven decades later, he was still trying. Nothing. It was like that man in that moment had never existed. But he did. And what he did in his moment will last forever.

The King shall look unto those on his right hand. Come, ye blessed of my Father, inherit the kingdom prepared for you from the foundation of the world:

For I was boy, trapped by hardship and thirsty to learn, and ye taught me and gave me drink. I was a stranger, broken and bleeding and ye carried me. I was sick and dying and ye visited me with cards and laughter and tended me.

Then shall Miss Smith and nameless marines and Dr. ?

answer him, saying, Lord, when saw we thee unlearned and taught thee, or broken and carried thee, or dying and tended thee?

And the King shall answer and say unto them, Verily I say unto you, Inasmuch as ye have done it unto one of the least of these, ye have done it unto me.

It is a glorious and terrifying thought. We touch many stories. We are touched by many stories. Miss Smith never saw the end of what she started. Those marines never knew what happened to the bloody pilot they carried to the last escaping plane. That medic saved a man and a leg without reading the rest of the book. He may have been killed. He may have simply moved on to the next man and the next leg.

But what they did, they did unto the King (because they did it unto his brethren). And they tipped tremendous scales as they did it, shaping lives and generations in ways that can never be undone.

A ten-year-old boy. An insecure girl. A lonely neighbor. Anyone thirsty. Anyone hungry or sick. Lives and generations and history are there for the tipping. You have hands. You have words. You have something. Touch the scales. Touch the least of these.

℘

The cargo that I carry down off of this mountain in these six sleepers is beyond comprehension. God has put eternity in our hearts—we have a sense of bigness—but no one can see all that He does from beginning to end. The five young souls closest to me are the first that I touch, and they are brothers and sisters to a King. He treasures them more than I ever could, even at my most wistful. He shaped them from nothing. He called them here and burdened them with me for a father. He beats their hearts and His breath inflates their lungs. He knows their beginnings and their ends. He knows how many other souls He will bring from these five in the centuries to come just as He knows how many flakes He hurled at me on the mountain. We are all flakes, hurled with intertwining artistry.

What I do unto these, I will have done unto Him.

Sweet relief erases my adrenaline like a scalding shower when we drop below the snow, when I carry my children into a tiny frigid motel room, wallpapered with the breath of a thousand smokers, as I tear up blankets and tuck kids in sideways on the bed like hotdog buns in a bag. The youngest is bundled into a battered crib. All of them unknowingly receive hands on their heads and parental prayers.

They passed through a storm that they will never see. Just as I have.

We were carried by marines while bombs fell. A young woman lifted our chins in a cornfield. We were healed by a man we can never meet and never thank.

But we can thank the One who sent him.

ELEVEN

Eyes Back: 3

NINE-YEAR-OLD JAMES WILSON WOKE UP ON SUNDAY mornings and brushed his hair, washed his face, put on his best, and walked off down the Nebraska country road toward a tiny (and in his words: "dead, dead, dead") Lutheran church.

The rest of the family slept.

They had all gone to church while staying with family in Seattle, and they had all benefited. But now, James was the only one trying to hang on to what he had felt in that church, to what he had smelled in those sermons and in that singing, to what he had almost begun to see.

It didn't last long. He went to church tired and alone and learned nothing (that he remembers). And he gave up.

He brawled and fought his way through junior high and high school. For two years, he worked the stockyards with the other teenage war-time cowboys, where they loaded twenty-two thousand head of cattle onto trains every day after school. Then, at the age of seventeen, James Wilson walked into a navy recruiter's office and enlisted.

It was the eighth of May 1945. That day, Germany surrendered.

He still felt unintelligent, though Miss Smith had caught him up in school long ago. When he studied, he felt like he was fooling people. He had learned the stars and the periodic table in order to "con" his high school science teachers. In the fleet, he entered as a Seaman First Class, because he managed to fool an entrance exam ("just some basic physics and gears and circuitry stuff"). From there, he applied to leave the fleet and enter a Naval Academy Prep School. He "fooled" a panel of officers into accepting him, and became one of twelve hundred sailors accepted. He might have thought of himself as dumb, but all of that "fooling" also made him feel smarter than everyone else. He was big, strong, competitive, and insecure. He had no friends, which he tried to tell himself was because he was better than everyone else at everything.

And then he received a letter. It was addressed to James Wilson, so he opened and read it.

It wasn't for him. And it was full of Bible verses—which he found embarrassing. He returned to sender.

And then another James Wilson knocked on his door. This James Wilson was tall and blond and athletic and educated and well-off and actually was better than everyone at everything. But everyone liked him anyway. He, too, had received some mail that was not his own.

The two James Wilsons became friends. Sort of. One of them was confident and carefree, and one of them was insecure and nervous and edgy and constantly keeping score, struggling to find any area in which he could feel like the superior human. He settled on the stars—after all, he'd used those effectively before.

One night, walking between buildings, one James looked up at the sky and nudged the other James. He began to name off the stars, feeling bigger and better about himself as he did.

The other James didn't care. He asked a question.

"Are you going to Heaven?"

My grandfather sneered. If he wasn't going, no one was. He figured he was about as good as people got. And then laughter, laughter that cut deep. His unthreatened friend assessed him honestly. He told him the truth. About everything.

And grace came.

Out of that little school, one James went off to Columbia. The other packed his bags for the Naval Academy. They were no longer friends—they were brothers.

My grandfather's faith grew at the Academy, and by the time he was an officer on the USS *Brush*, the first from his class sailing for the Korean War, he was as "born again" as they come. Which meant, on a ship of hard-drinking, gambling, whoring sailors (but I repeat myself), he was no longer a man bothered by laughter. He was well on his way to being the evangelist and pastor that he would become.

And then God gave him another story.

James Wilson was in the gunnery room, stationed below decks with his finger on the only trigger that fired every gun on that destroyer. For a while, freshly converted and naïve, he had become a pacifist. But no more. Now his finger was the one that flung the thunder.

The *Brush* was at battle stations, every man tied to his position until conflict had been cleared. No man, under any circumstances, was to leave his station. To do so would be considered desertion.

And then the gunnery officer of the USS *Brush* summoned Lt. James Wilson to an observation room above the bridge. My grandfather declined. While at battle stations, such summons were a distraction. His superior officer did not take this well. He ordered James up and James declined again. Finally, enough raging authority compelled James to leave his battle station. He pulled a man over, pushed him into his chair, gave him his headset, and climbed quickly up above decks, up past the bridge, and into the observation room.

James reported to the gunnery officer and asked why he was needed. The man had no idea. James turned to leave, but he was stopped. He asked permission to return to his battle station, but his superior forbade him. Lt. James Wilson was absolutely required to remain until further notice.

And then the USS *Brush* hit a mine. The impact was in the gunnery room. Fire. Smoke. A sinking ship. Bodies.

When I was young, my grandfather described for me what it was like when he had finally been dismissed. He hurried down metal stairs and raced to the hatch where sailors were pulling out bodies. And in that moment, all eyes were on him.

At first, he was a ghost. No man was ever away from his battle station. His charred body had already been pulled out. But there he stood. Living. Pardoned. Reserved for another purpose.

As that ship limped toward port without much hope, racing the flood of seawater in its hull, running pumps without ceasing, as they named those in the crew who had died, the story of James Wilson spread.

He had been pulled to safety. On a hunch. For no reason.

And James discovered that he wasn't there to fight. He was there to fish.

He began preaching. He still hasn't stopped.

The fire of the gospel burned faster than the water flooded in, and a hobbled destroyer with a very different crew just managed to make port.

Somewhere, there is a sailor who died for me.

TWELVE

City Hiatus: London

I HAVE BEEN HERE BEFORE, BUT NEVER ALONE. I'M NOT sure why I'm here now. I am going where I am told, wherever this crew with cameras might need me to stand and smile and chat. My wife shooed me into this, but I have left her with our youngest joy, only six days old. I would like to be home. But I am not. I am here and we are not filming. Yet. Anytime now. Maybe.

Which is why I am walking the city instead of sitting on a bus on its way to Oxford where my sister and her family live in a stone cottage at the end of a little lane that crosses a picturesque stream with an appetite for stolen bicycles. I have nephews and nieces there. I could be sitting in that kitchen or in that living room, drinking American coffee and looking out the window at cows grazing on the mounded stripe that marks the buried Roman road. I could be with my sister, or metal-detecting with her kids. I could be with my brother-in-law in the most glorious rare book collection I ever expect to see and smell and wander. Last time, I asked for a first printing of Spenser's *Faerie Queene*. And they handed it to me—a book twice as old as my country and crowded full of quill-scratched annotations and marginalia. I had needed it, you see. For research. For a novel. For children.

None of that this time. I am on my own, in London almost by accident, and in no mood to see the sights (though I could go for some sites).

I am replaying history in my head as I walk the streets, finding horrible gaps in my memory. Trying to sort out and see the layers in this town's incredible life. Paganism of the deepest, darkest stripe. The Romans and their roads and their sewers. The first bridge builders and their human sacrifices. Skipping, skipping, the Empire. Hopping over that glitch with my own rambunctious colony. The industrial crush. The fog that was no fog at all, but the constant lung-killing belch of smokestacks. The religious hypocrisies. The Dickensian hypocrisies. The power and the loss of power. One lost generation and then another. Nazi bombs.

This is a town where digging is dangerous. Viking graves and Saxon graves and Roman graves and Norman graves could ruin anyone's dreams of a cellar. But even though I think of this town in terms of its dead, in terms of its past, it *is* still living. It is still crowded with the living.

I descend into the white-tiled tube and watch an immigrant beating his rhythms on a bucket. I ride this crowded underworld train and rise up the long escalators toward the light. I emerge and watch red buses crowded with tourists here to see the flashing billboards now mounted on the headstone that marks the grave of Londontown, and where London still tips more of the world's story than Americans know. We treat London like it's entirely museum, like it's all deadwood on the tree from which we've sprung. I sit by the cutesy bronze statue of Eros and I think about the dead and the living and pints and meat pasties, about all that this town has seen, and I wonder how much more it will see. Much is buried here. And where much is buried, much will grow. There are ages still unwritten for this place. In four hundred years, will there be red buses? Will there be an America from which Americans can come and be confused by this city stacked with history? From that distance, squinting through ignorance at the past, will they wonder if Henry VIII came after Victoria or before? Will there yet be new zeniths to be compared to the old?

London has died before, and London has been reborn. And London has died.

A Japanese couple approaches me, extending wide smiles and nods and a camera. They stand in front of the cherubic devil, Eros, loving each other. Showing me their love so that I might capture it, so that I might digitally capture and digitally store a file that imitates the way in which bright starlight (from our sun) is rippling off of them in this moment in time. So that they might remember.

I do. And I know that their story winds back as far as this city's, back to the beginning, back to when the first words became the first light. I hand them their memory and smile. They leave, driving their story forward, walking a thread that might last a day and might last millennia, a thread that could outrun cities.

Night falls, but the little film crew that has brought me here has done no filming. I pace my story back to a hotel, not thinking about opportunities missed, not wishing to have been elsewhere. I was here. I was given scenes, and I was meant to live them well. My collar is up and cold hands clench in my pockets.

In a warm hotel room overlooking this city, I should sleep. But I am from another side of this planet, where the sun is up and my wife is holding my child. The clock marches and marches and my mind marches with it, savoring this strange, unexpected day. I cannot sleep. I test my window and find that it opens. A large ledge waits for me outside and I slip out onto it, pressing my back against stone and bracing my feet. The brick quivers as a barely audible underworld train passes beneath us. The city stretches away from me, not at all like a patient etherized on a table. It is a ruin and a graveyard. And it is neither. Well-lit construction cranes and millions of souls sprout from composted history, and they all march this story forward.

Sitting on that ledge, I dig out my phone, and I throw my voice around the world to my wife. I send her a poem.

Londontown

Entombed trains shiver my stones
racing from grave to grave.
Romans and Saxons and Normans,
deep locked and rotten all,
have grown used to the express,
to this invasion by the living hordes,
and herds.
The dead point me toward Picadilly
from behind white tiles,
and beneath this man
playing his bucket.
Lazarus stairs
carry me to the resurrection,
to a bronze god on his fountain,
and the duties of the living.
So I smile and nod and photograph
the eager Japanese.

THIRTEEN

Rules for Mortals

HINT: THERE'S TWO.

The long living room with the cracked plaster walls had never changed. Chairs had been moved here and there, the old couches that my grandfather used to flip up and push together into forts were long gone. But the rest was the same.

This golden-brown carpet has been on this floor longer than I have been alive. I know what it feels like beneath socked feet; I know its texture beneath my hands and against my cheek. I slept on it beside that old fireplace every New Year's Eve.

The pictures on the piano and the mantel are the same (though new ones have joined the collection). The curving, carpeted attic stairs are just as they were when I lived in that attic after our house fire, and I have older memories of them as well—memories of a small boy leaping off from higher and higher steps while my grandmother worried and my grandfather laughed.

I watched the first rounds of Desert Storm on that television. I put in long hours beside my grandmother, watching *Jeopardy*. I even read some of her Christian romance novels plucked from stacks on the upper attic stairs.

The attic still smells like knotty pine and dust, and the brick chimney still heats it like a furnace.

I lived in this house. I loved this house. But I loved what it held far more.

My wry grandmother in a pull-over apron, yellow rubber hands in dishwater. My ever humming and hymning grandfather. A cracked green cookie jar full of Fig Newtons more often than not. My grandmother's Canadian loyalty to the queen.

On one fall day, I ate pork chops and stewed apples in this house, and it was a revelation.

I climbed the low sprawling apple trees in the backyard and beat on the punching bag in the little broken-down shed and inhaled plums and watched my grandfather fill a Nebraska yearning in his soul by planting short rows of corn.

I brought my future wife here to meet my ancestors and receive their overflowing love. My grandmother glowed, eyes sparkling, lips pursed.

"Oh, she's lovely."

I bent down for my hug, and got a kiss and a whispered

command to keep this lovely girl with the blue eyes and the wild hair.

In this living room, I brought our first son to sit at the feet of our Lady Wisdom, and he stole her walker instead, staggering around behind it in his snug overalls. I brought our first daughter to sit with her great-grandmother on this couch and receive kisses and admiration and compliments on her curls, her huge eyes, her looping lashes.

In this house, my grandmother was renamed by small Wilson children.

A girl from the Canadian prairie, who had lost her brothers in war, who had been fatherless when she met her Father in a tent meeting, who had gone to Japan after the war, armed with the gospel and forgiveness, who had met a tall, young naval officer and had done everything she could to discourage him—that girl grew old with living and sat in this room, and decades fell off of her memory as she looked upon the children of her grandson, and she began to sing. She sang the same song every time my children appeared.

The song was Japanese. It was about little sparrows.

Chi chi pa pa chi pa pa
Susume no gakko no sensei wa
Muchi o furi furi chi pa pa
Chi chi pa pa chi pa pa.

She became Grandma Chi-chi-pa.

She is not on the couch now, watching her *Jeopardy*. She

is not up to her elbows in dishwater or steeping her tea or filling the cookie jar.

She is in the back bedroom, lost in a deeper sleep.

Not long before, she met our youngest. Marisol—our little sunny sea. My grandmother held my daughter. She was afraid to, but I gave her no choice, and I supported her arms.

This time, I lead five children back to where my grandfather keeps his constant watch—to where he sings to this sleeper, to where he read her the New Testament (twice) as she faded, to where he listened to her speak to people he could not see.

Her face is changed, smooth and taut. She is breathing hard and steady, like a woman running a race. Because she is. Because she is in her final push, nearing the line while we sit in the stands.

The fear was hard at first, but her husband and others that only she could see were there. Her brother Jack? Her dearest friend Dotty? I couldn't say what a faithful daughter may or may not see as she nears the end, but I am no unbeliever. This world is more than a meaningless storm of meaningless matter. We are as much creatures after death as we were before—why would we not be given tasks? Why would we be kept back from the harvest of loved souls?

God is a God of galaxies, of storms, of roaring seas and boiling thunder, but He is also the God of bread baking, of a child's smile, of dust motes in the sun. He is who He is, and always shall be. Look around you now. He is speaking always and everywhere. His personality can be seen and known and leaned upon. The sun is belching flares while mountains scrape our sky while ants are milking aphids on their colonial leaves and dolphins are laughing in the surf and wheat is rippling and wind is whipping and a boy is looking into the eyes of a girl and mortals are dying.

The God who looked on you with joy when you were small and racing across His gift of green grass on His gift of feet beneath His gift of sky watched by His gift of a mother with His gift of love in His gift of her eyes, is the same God who will look on you as that race finally ends. He is the same, but we have changed, between our opening lines and our final page.

We cannot see every moment of our own stories, let alone any other mortal story. None of us even have first-hand knowledge of our own early years of existence—what we think we know is all taken on faith.

But God has been there every second. He has crafted every step and gesture and breath of every mortal you have ever passed, of every driver on every road that has ever flicked by you at night, of every kicking child in every mall. And He will be there when we end.

When our time comes, God will be as kind and as generous and as raucous and as deft as He ever and always is.

We are mortals. We are seeds grown and hardened for planting, intended for the ground, and for a glorious Easter harvest after. The first Reaper is a foe, rending soul from flesh, and oh, how we run from him, how we stop our breathing and cower behind locked doors in our mortal darkness. But when our Brother takes up the scythe, there will be drums and sun and sweat mixed with laughter. Then we will beg not to be Passed Over.

We are mortals. We should know our role.

We are characters—spoken and shaped down to the rhythms of the electrons in our toe fungus. But we are also active. We have been shaped in the Shaper's image.

We are creators.

Look around. Can you see time flowing past your edges? Can you see the future breaking around you and becoming the past?

Does that thing we call *now* exist? Is there actually a present, an empty moment in which the future is not and the past is not? Can you find the edge of the shadow of a speeding car? Sure. Just tell me when and I'll freeze the frame. The problem is that *when* is the speeding car.

Truth: We are the present. We are now. We are the razor's edge of history. The future flies at us and from that dark blur we shape the past.

And the past is forever.

We are authors and we are writing every second of every day. A child scissors a couch, and that action is forever and always. It cannot be undone. But now it is your turn. What you say and what you do in response will be done forever, never to be appealed, edited, or modified.

If life is a race (and it is), then it is run across wet concrete.

If life is a story (and it is), then that story is the cumulative spatter of our tracks.

Write a novel in real time, without a glance back over your shoulder. Shape children in real time, without a glance back. This is terrifying.

Of course, we try to edit. We dump lies and lies of whiteout behind us. We are always explaining and attempting to recast our actions in "better light." Did you not see that child scissoring my couch? God wanted me to yell and glare and grip that small wrist far more tightly than was necessary. Justice. Righteousness.

Oh?

We are mortals engaged in high-speed creation. Perhaps some guidelines would be useful. My kingdom for some rules of thumb.

Forgive us our trespasses as we forgive those who trespass against us.

%^&**!

Seriously? We are supposed to pray that line? Who among us can truly make that request to God without both knees buckling? Are you ready to ask God to deal with you only as graciously as you deal with others?

But she totally lied about me.

But he's been mooching my groceries.

But . . .

But . . .

Sure. You've been wronged. Now show God how you would like Him to treat you when you're the one doing wrong.

Rule 1 for Mortals: Love the Lord your God (with every bit of you).

Rule 2 for Mortals: Love your neighbor as yourself.

Tip 1 for Mortals: Ask God to call your bluffs.

Living means decisions. Living means writing your every word and action and thought and drool spot down in *forever*. It means writing your story within the Story. It means being terrible at it. It means failing and knowing that, somehow, all of our messes will still contribute, that the creative God has merely given Himself a greater challenge—drawing glory from our clumsy botching of the past. We are like factory workers in a slapstick comedy, standing at our positions beside the too-fast conveyor belt that flings the future and all of our possible actions at us. Corn syrup and food coloring everywhere (along with cheese and ceramic figurines).

Do your best. Live. Create. Fail.

How many thieves can we fit on this cross?

How many of us can be dead in Lazarus's tomb?

Is there room for more dry bones in this valley? Because I could lie down.

I can complain in a wilderness.

Or maybe deny Christ three times?

Resent the righteous?

Shoo away some children?

Fail to grow figs?

Panic in a storm?

Forget God's law?

Pursue my lusts?

Sell out my Maker?

Hang myself in a field?

So glad I could help.

And from it all, from the compost of our efforts, God brings glory—a world of ripe grain in the wind.

By His grace, we are the water made wine. We are the dust made flesh made dust made flesh again. We are the whores made brides and the thieves made saints and the killers made apostles. We are the dead made living.

We are His cross.

❧

As my grandfather watches, I lift each of my children up to kiss their Chi-chi-pa. Her fast breathing doesn't slow. My turn comes and her head is hot to my touch—hot with effort.

But this isn't sickness. There is no disease here.

This is what living looks like.

When it ends.

We will sing on a hilltop, beside a box, above a hole.

In a few days, I will be asked to stand in a sanctuary and scatter words at this life. Along with other grandsons, I will look out at remaining mortals and use my allotted two minutes to honor my father's mother as best I can. Two minutes or two days, there's not enough time.

There never is. But the finish line gives us focus.

In Memoriam: Elizabeth Catherine

The hole has been dug and filled. The sod mounds where we placed you, well out of the shade, crowning the hill. You did not belong in a valley. You are gone, as gone as anyone can be, but I will not grieve for you selfishly.

I hope.

Death came slowly here, disguised as age, creeping up over decades and only you seemed to believe it was coming. You smelled it. You promised the rest of us, and we laughed. You were like a child, insisting that you had grown—that four was big, that six, that ten was as old and aged as anyone could be. And still more years came.

But now you have grown. You are where you have always wanted to be. And we are here, after decades of your warnings, somehow still surprised at death's arrival.

You were the soul of the yellow house on Howard. You were the wry fire that kept its insides warm. I climbed in your apple trees and in your walls, and you plied me with toffees and half-smiling quips. You were and are mother to my father—the tree from which apples fell and grew from which apples fell and grew from which apples now fall and grow. You are gone from this orchard, but I and my sisters and cousins and many others will grow on, pointing toward the Son you showed us. We will live—and we will die—in Christ, thankful that He placed us downstream in the river of your human grace.

And Amen.

FOURTEEN

Eyes Back: 4

HERE I AM, SON OF MANY. HERE SHE IS, DAUGHTER OF MANY.

I have been carried to this moment by lives unseen, by men and women unthanked. By grace. The same wind carried her.

We are two motes in the sun, and now we swirl together, beginning something, feeling like the founders of the human race, like the opening page of the opening chapter of the first story ever told.

We are fools. But we are supposed to be. We are one of the great mysteries that puzzled Solomon. A mystery just a few days younger than the world itself: boy meets girl.

Love widened my senses. It made me a sponge for tastes and tones and moments. I grabbed for them all like a man drowning—because I was.

I gave the girl a ring that had belonged to my mother's mother's mother. She took it. We swore oaths and people watched. We tangled our stories into one. We made our words flesh. Till death do us part, we will run in stride and shoulder loads and shoulder laughter and shape new layers of the past.

And visit the ocean as often as possible.

 ℰ

An old memory, first written when it was fresh.

The moment was thick with its own reality. It slowed down and sank in.

It ached merrily. Did my wife feel it too? She smiled at me, feeling it and something extra. She had the moment and me along with it—a jester to go with the joke.

Big sky. Cold sand. Tightening toes. A warm hand in mine. A warm life in mine.

I stopped and struggled to absorb. It should have been as thick as fudge, gumming me up and making me thirsty, but it wasn't. Instead I stood stretching for it, reaching with every physical and spiritual nerve available trying to feel the reality of the sand beneath my feet, the surf grabbing at birds behind me, the blank sky above, the inlet before, the lighthouse flicking in nervous anticipation of the black, thundering sky armies that were swallowing the horizon. I stood with my back to the sea, wanting to be overwhelmed.

Stillness wasn't working. My feet moved, and I turned to search for my smallness further out.

Packs of birds ran from the motion of my feet. They ran from the feet of the ocean. Up and down the banked sand they raced, never overwhelmed, never washed out, up to their bird knees and then out again and back in. Froth licked their feathers but could not cling to their speed. They were frantic sheep in a frantic herd, waiting for something from the sea. They searched the beach in front of me for a drowned friend. Bird chief? Master? Dogs then, not sheep. This pack of Argus birds awaited their Odysseus, their Jonah spat up by the great fish.

I grew weary of their constancy and ran at them.

The sandbar peninsula crawled out into the ocean before it grew fearful and hooked back to run alongside the shore. Along its serpentine back were spines, the gleanings of storms and tides, gathered and piled by gloved hands, as if for burning. The cold sand swallowed my feet while I pushed my way up the sandbar toward the sea's rejected.

Boy: Are you coming?

Girl: I am watching.

An offshore wind, vanguard to the storm, swam around me when I crested the bank and looked down on the small inlet captured by the hook peninsula. Beside me towered driftwood strung with torn nets, sheltering trash thrown beneath—one rubber glove, buckets, cork, Styrofoam. The beams to this hall were the shattered and smoothed bones of trees, the tarred and heavy ties of railroads and one sign. The post of the sign was at least twelve feet, long enough to plant deep in sand, deep enough to survive storms. Its face was of wood, but blank. My hand could not quite surround the post, and my arm struggled to free it from the others.

The wind pulled at me, I pulled at the post, and we both came loose. The pile shifted when the sign came away, but it did not fall. It was heavy for my hand, but I turned and held it up toward the storm, trying to think of something to say. There were no words, so I laughed and leaned the head of my long sign against the wind stronger than man's hand— and the gusts helped support it. In the water of the inlet, the torsos of two men were fishing, unaware of the blessing my rod benedicted above their heads and backs.

My Moses arm grew weary and sank beneath the weight of my sign, even with the help of the wind. The post once again met sand. The armies of the storm grew blacker, faster in their pace, charging the sea. I worried for the fishermen, and watched as lightning began to flick. The sky above and behind me was still blue, but darkening. Not darkening because of the storm, not just yet, but by the force of evening. The sun was dropping, hidden by rumbling clouds.

I threw away my defeated staff and walked on. There were other spines on this sandbar's back.

The birds still ran in the foam, ignoring the storm, faithful to whatever the sea had stolen. I picked up a rock and threw it at the pack. It hopped into the arms of the ocean. A seagull flew past me. It held a crab in its mouth, pulled from the inlet, legs moving, clanking. The gull dropped it and landed. The crab was flipped quickly onto its back, its breastplate removed, and its insides eaten. The legs still moved, but slower now. I threw another rock. The gull flew, and I found myself standing over the still-struggling remains. Present for the very embrace of death, I watched. Here was my smallness. Death came, death must have come, but still the legs moved. The jerks slowed and stopped. I pushed sand over the crab with my foot, and looked to the coming war.

The world erupted.

The clouds met their enemy; he burst from beneath them. The blackness had marched too high, well overhead now, and the sun had brought itself low, lower than they. He burst, hugging the earth and ripping at the bottoms of the clouds. Red. I had not seen red before. Clouds with small lightning, finger-tip sparks, could not match his wrath. Their blackness was nothing more than canvas for his fire. I stood and watched that fire grow. Fire from the heavens now springs from earth. Dragons get their bellies burned.

But it was too much. The world would be swallowed, scorched; it could not survive this painting without a frame. I squatted, looking for some boundary, some cork for this bottle, anything that could hold it, make it drinkable, contain it, prevent it from smothering reality. I brought the lighthouse against the sun, but it was eaten, torn down, and trampled. The houses, the cliff, the fisherman, they stood, their blackness together could stand. But the sun grew bigger, shone beneath the clouds, shone off the clouds, ran all over the ground and up.

The fishermen were eaten by an inlet of fire. I looked to the Argus birds. They had fled, fled or found the one they waited on. Then I looked for my post, the sign stripped of words, undug by the sea. I ran to it.

I drove it deep in the sand and stepped back. The explosion of light poured around it. I sat and it touched the sun. I crawled onto my belly. The sun was swallowed by the stake.

The painting had a wooden frame. My wife was laughing. She is laughing. She has not stopped. We ran from the darting sunlit rains and the lightning and the night.

We haven't stopped running, but we are getting slower. We have little people running with us now. We have passed others. Our own people will pass us. They will grow and meet others who are young and strong and they will feel as if they are part of the very beginning of life.

We may fall on our knees or into a final sleep, but we will see the inside of that storm. We will see the other side of that storm, where there is no death from living.

The young will mark the sand with a stone and gather round to scatter words on the wind and ponder the speed of time, of life, of grace.

I do it now.

In Memoriam: Lawrence Aubry

We plant a man. We plant him in a garden reserved for such men. The soil is right for him here, in this place of flags, of ranks, of service pride, in this place where the mournful horn blows and old hands salute.

When the great Easter comes to *this* garden, to *this* sun-filled field, when the horns of final triumph blow, the crop here will be soldiers, sailors, marines . . . and the men who wore wings. And you, Granddad, among them.

Strong hands, strong heart, strong will—you were cut from the toughest cloth of a generation, cloth that wouldn't tear or give, perfect for flight suits and coveralls and combat and war. That toughness could struggle in homes, on sofas, in the soft places, but that toughness saved the world.

You, Granddad, had seen Death before. You had felt its breath on you, that cold wind that tugs soul from flesh. Engines quitting high in the sky, bullets gnawing wings, fallen friends, shredded planes, and on the ground—bombs. The bomb that threw you and chewed your leg. The sizzling shrapnel you brushed off your chest. For a while, your life was simply *almost death*. You knew fear, terror even, but you never broke. Not then.

I was young, and I stood there, feet in the water, watching you stride into the lake, demanding to be baptized. I watched you sink. I watched you rise again, walking out of your own Jordan with two fists raised and a whoop of triumph. I listened to you tell me, tell everyone, and all the world, "Praise the Lord." You were broken, but not by bullets and bombs. You were broken by grace.

Once more you have walked out into the water. Once more, I watch you sink. May we have your courage, for we will sink too—your children and grandchildren and descendants unborn. But we serve the Man who was planted, the Son who rose, who gave you to us and us to you. And when He calls, we will rise together and raise our fists and whoop while the horns blow and drums roll and banners curl in the sky like ticker tape for the great parade.

Until then, we hope, we pray, we plant a man.

You, Granddad, fly ahead.

Your last war is won.

FIFTEEN

Moses, Keep Your Hands Up

THERE WAS A MAN WHO CAME DOWN A MOUNTAIN. HIS FACE was glowing and his hands were full (of words made stone).

He dropped those hands. He dropped those stones. And when he did, destruction.

He got new stones, and when he raised his hands again, he was giving hope and granting strength. But those arms were heavy. While battle raged, men came and held up his arms. If those hands dropped, destruction.

Can you see him there? Standing above the struggle, a man with his arms out? Does it look familiar?

Moses parted the Red Sea. He called down Death. He slipped off his sandals and met with God. But he couldn't keep his hands up. That weight on his arms was heavier than plagues, than a people, than Egypt.

There was a man strong enough to bare-hand lions, who needed only a jawbone to face armies. That man's hands tore city gates off of hinges and bound fire to foxes. He triumphed all the way into defeat. He was broken and blinded—enslaved.

Until a boy helped him put his hands up.

Who does Samson look like, standing there with his head down and those arms stretched out, touching stones? And when they dropped, destruction.

Moses was poured out. Samson was spent. Two men who pulled down worlds.

There was a Man who could walk on water. He could raise the dead and heal with a touch. He became Samson—armed with an ox-goad against thousands. He became Moses, turning water into blood (of blessing).

But He came to raise His arms, to get His hands up. Load those shoulders with the world. Put those law stones in His hands. And if they drop, destruction.

No boy came to guide His hands. No men to prop Him up. His arms were braced with nails.

He was pierced and scourged and mocked. He was cursed and raised up on a tree, but He was in that ancient pose of victory.

An old man on a hill, a blind man between two pillars, the God Man on a cross.

Glory is sacrifice, glory is exhaustion, glory is having nothing left to give.

Almost.

It is death by living.

The earth shook. The roof came down. The world changed. The armies fled.

That Moses kept his hands up.

e⤳

I was laughing with my kids, driving through a college campus on our way home. And I saw someone in the distance that had to be James I. Wilson. Who else would be sitting behind a small folding table in suspenders and a tie, with his cane beside him, and free books in front of him?

He was positioned in the grass between three large dorms—an old man out fishing. Three people were circling his canoe, and I could see that he was laughing.

He has something left. A few ounces more to give. And a few more. And a few more.

He is a reminder.

To get my hands up. To grope for the pillars. To saddle up the mustang and hang on tight. To live for this woman who is giving her life for me, for these little humans who are our love made flesh. Ride the roaring wave of providence with eager expectation. To search for the stories all around me. To see Christ in every pair of eyes. To write a past I won't regret. To reach the dregs of the life I've been given and then to lick the bottom of my mug. To live hard and die grateful.

And to enjoy it.

SIXTEEN

City Hiatus: Home

I LOWER MYSELF ONTO A HARDWOOD FLOOR TO STRETCH. The little finger on my left hand pops where I once snapped it sideways in high school. On my right hand, my ring finger is permanently twisted (courtesy of a soccer goalpost long ago). Half of my left knee has been numb since I was seventeen (courtesy of football). My nose angles to the right (courtesy of a friend's gloved fist). I haven't been able to open my jaw without cracking it since at least junior high. A scar stripes my forearm where a friend's fingernail dug a long trough in eighth grade (football). Three years ago, surgeons drilled through my spine and scraped splattered cartilage off of nerve bundles that ran into my legs. Nerves still tingle in my right hand where I once took a knife blade.

The war wounds of an average life.

I was up all night, writing too long. And now another day is ending. The floor is a luxury. I stretch my arms above my head, and my spine drums a brisk percussion of adjustment from top to bottom.

And sunlight slides into the front window—slicing sideways through my living room as the huge fire in the sky descends.

Motes of dust are suddenly visible, floating in the gold. Galaxies.

There is nothing new under the sun. There we all are. Dust. Floating on grace. Beautiful only in its light.

And I am taken everywhere at once.

A friend went to Kurdistan to teach English—and to carry grace. As he prayed in a classroom, a gun was put to his head. And then he saw the face of God.

A childhood friend took another man's patrol in Fallujah. He fell for another like a sailor once fell for my own grandfather.

I think about a cousin and a nephew and a teammate and a high school classmate and the millions of brothers and sisters who have been carried on the same gold that now holds me—who rode on the grace of time, who were given tastes and touches and yearnings. Who had eternity in their dust mote hearts and have now gone closer to the sun.

There, on the floor, I am grasping. Trying to find words. Trying to use words to mine thoughts. And then I am saved.

Mari has identified her vulnerable father. I hear galloping

two-year-old feet and I contract my core in preparation. Laughing, she careens through the sun. Dust swirls and I am surprised to see her notice. She pauses and turns back around, freezing, crouching, watching the golden worlds. And then she attacks.

"Shoo!" Arms flap. She hops. "Shoo! Go away! Go home!" She attacks the dust. She does dancing battle in the sun. As should we all.

It ends as quickly as it began. Her philosophy complete, she throws herself onto me, rib to rib, dust to dust.

Life is here. Life is now.

Gratitude

Matt Baugher for his patience.

My Lovely for her tears and her laughter.

My many careening ancestors for their careening.

My parents for every forgotten meal and every
forgotten story.

Unknown marines for carrying a broken pilot.

Unknown sailor for dying in the place of many
Wilsons.

Miss Smith for teaching a boy in a cornfield.

My granddad for his stories lived and told.

My grandfather for his faithful fishing.

My grandmother for her son, my father.

My grandmother for her daughter, my mother.

My Author, for the star that burns my face, for
grace, for breath, for every kicking beat within
my chest, for the Son who kept His hands
up, for the people I am meant to live myself
to death for. For bigness. For smallness. For
bread. For wine. For all they represent.

About the Author

N. D. WILSON IS A BEST-SELLING AUTHOR, PROFESSIONAL daydreamer, and occasional screenwriter. His novels include the 100 Cupboards trilogy and the Ashtown Burials series; his first work of nonfiction was *Notes from the Tilt-A-Whirl*, and he has several scripts in various stages of development.

He enjoys hilltops, calluses, and the smell of rain on hot asphalt. He and his wife have five children, and they watch them battle the sea with surfboards and buckets as often as possible. He once faked the Shroud of Turin, which got him yelled at on Hungarian television, and he typed a tiny novel on a paper napkin which was then printed in *Esquire* magazine (that bastion of righteousness). He is currently a Fellow of Literature at New Saint Andrews College, where he teaches freshmen how to play with words. Like everyone else, he is made from dust.